Enslaved Realities in Ancient Palestine

Elisa Kozey

ABSTRACT

This project examines the epigraphic, archaeological and literary evidence for slavery in first century CE Palestine. Detailed knowledge of slavery practices in this period is critical for the understanding of historical and religious texts of the second temple period, as slavery in Palestine differed from other parts of the empire. When taken together, extant evidence shows that first century Palestinian slavery served to reinforce the political, military and religious status quo by providing autonomy from the broader subjugated population.

Table of Contents

Table of Contents v
List of Tables vi
List of Figures vii
Chapter 2: Method 12
Chapter 3: Epigraphic Evidence 28
Chapter 4: Archaeological Evidence 44
Chapter 5: Literary Evidence 54
Chapter 6: Conclusions 83

Chapter 1: Introduction

In his cross-cultural analysis of slavery in early Greece, the historian and sociologist Orlando Patterson first makes note of the "tantalizing shortage of data" on the subject of slavery in the ancient world, writing "Clio has been especially cruel to classical historians, giving them just enough information to confirm slavery was important in many ancient states but not enough to go beyond informed guesses."[1] There is little doubt about the overall importance of the institution in the economic, political, community and family life of the first century CE Mediterranean, the setting for both my present study. Slavery was everywhere in the Roman world; one estimate puts the total number of enslaved persons at 10 million out of the total imperial population of 50 million during that period.[2] Still, significant questions remain. For Patterson, one such question is why the institution took on a particular importance and intensity in this time period. He writes that, while "slavery as an institutionalized micro-sociological relation of domination has existed throughout the world," only a handful of cultures have developed the practice to the point that "its removal would have entailed critical dislocations in the society at large," a characteristic of what he, following Moses Finley, calls a "genuine slave society."[3] The process of latifundialization

---

[1] Orlando Patterson, "Slavery, Gender, and Work in the Pre-Modern World and Early Greece: A Cross-Cultural Analysis," in *Slave Systems: Ancient and Modern*, eds. Enrico Dal Lago and Constantina Katsari (Cambridge: Cambridge University Press, 2008), 32.
[2] Keith Bradley, "On the Roman Slave Supply and Slavebreeding." in *Classical Slavery*, ed. Moses Finley (London, F. Cass, 1987), 42.
[3] Patterson, 33.

and military conquest described by Keith Hopkins in his book *Conquerors and Slaves: Sociological Studies in Roman History*, a more-or-less constant cycle of "continuous war, the influx of booty [including slaves], its investment in land, the formation of large estates, the impoverishment of peasants, their emigration to towns and the provinces and the growth of urban markets,"[4] which was repeated throughout the imperial period, undoubtedly entrenched existing traditional practices of slavery on the Italian peninsula, while giving them an international character and scale.[5]

First century Palestine existed at the periphery of this empire, steeped in the cultural legacy of the ancient Near East and in the memories of its own independent religious and political traditions. The region was Hellenized during the conquest of Alexander in the fourth century BCE, and alternated between Ptolemaic and Seleucid rule, either directly or through Maccabean client kings. The Jewish law codified in the Hebrew Bible condoned enslavement of both fellow Jews and foreigners, and there is limited archaeological evidence for its continued practice in the Hellenistic period.[6] By the beginning of the first century, Roman influence in the region was already firmly entrenched, accompanied by an imperial political and military presence and, after the demise of the Herodian dynasty, the introduction of Roman law. These changes impacted the function of slavery within Palestine, even as the region became a source of slaves for

---

[4] Keith Hopkins, *Conquerors and Slaves: Sociological Studies in Roman History* (Cambridge, UK: Cambridge University Press, 1977), 11.
[5] For which there was already criticism in antiquity. Of the process Pliny writes in *HN* 18.35, verumque confitentibus latifundia perdidere Italiam, iam vero et provincias, "if the truth is confessed, latifundia have been the ruin of Italy, now it also true of the provinces."
[6] One such example is a Hellenistic inscription from Maresha, which Esther Eshel interprets as a diplomatic inscription referencing "'DRTW one of B'WŠW, a slave," עדרתו חד מן אבאושו עבדה. See Esther. "Inscriptions in Hebrew, Aramaic and Phoenician Script," in *Maresha Excavations Final Report III, 35–88, (IAA Reports 45)* (Jerusalem: Israel Antiquities Authority, 2010), 63.

export to Rome. This thesis examines the extent to which slaveholding practices from the broader Roman empire penetrated the Palestinian society of the first century CE. In brief, I will show that in contrast to Rome itself, which was a 'slave society' marked by near total economic and social dependence on the institution, slavery in early Roman Palestine served largely to provide autonomy and security to the ruling class of Roman occupiers and their local collaborators. While there is some evidence for the use of slaves in domestic, agricultural and light industrial activity, the preponderance of epigraphic, archaeological and literary evidence shows a strong connectivity either with the elite Herodian and priestly families and with the foreign presence in the region.

What follows is comprised of six parts. In the remainder of this chapter, I discuss the state of current scholarship on Roman slavery that has relevance for first century Palestine, as well as some of the ideological and practical challenges in examining historical questions about the region. Chapter two, "Method," examines the approaches taken various scholars to the presence and absence of evidence for slavery in the material record. Chapter three, "Epigraphy," examines five inscriptions from early Roman Palestine, each of which illustrates a dimension of the slave system at work in the region and greater empire. Chapter four, "Archaeological Evidence," applies theories and interpretive methods formulated from elite domestic slavery in other parts of the empire to the priestly mansions of Jerusalem's Herodian Quarter, including the "Burnt House" and "Mansion House." Chapter five, "Textual Evidence," looks at literary evidence to illustrate attitudes and practices specific to the context of first century Palestine, including examples from the New Testament, the works of Josephus and first century traditions preserved in the

Mishnah. Finally, I offer some conclusions about the practice of slavery in world of first century Palestinians, returning to the question of its function and social location.

This project is not without scholarly challenges, however. Jennifer Glancy writes that, while "a wide variety of sources attests to the contours of slavery in the Roman Empire, from bills of sale to legal codes and literary works," nonetheless "any description of slavery in antiquity is the product of multiple scholarly decisions," including the weight given to particular categories of evidence and the connections between texts and their historical contexts.[7] The presence of multiple strands of evidence can even form a kind of trap, one that presents a false sense of "concreteness" and a "seamless picture of ancient life" that conceals disparities or gaps in the evidence.[8] Glancy's warnings weigh on this project in two distinct ways. First, there is the question of how applicable the economic, legal and social practice of slavery documented in other parts of the empire, and especially Italy and the Greek city states, is for our understanding of first century Israel. Israel was without question a fully integrated part of the Roman world; nonetheless it was a part that prided itself on its cultural, religious and ethical distinctiveness. Secondly, there is the question of whether the categories of evidence presented, which include religious and non-religious texts, epigraphic and archaeological evidence, are coherent enough to reveal the specificities of slavery as it was practiced in first century Israel.

Scholarly hesitance presents its own set of challenges, though. As Sandra Joshel and Lauren Petersen point out, our modern fixation with absolute coherence and certainty risks re-inscribing the prejudices and silences imposed on the archaeological and literary record

---

[7] Jennifer A. Glancy, *Slavery in Early Christianity* (New York: Oxford University Press, 2002), 3-4.
[8] Ibid.

by persons of elite social status, who were the primary cultural producers and, in most instances, slave owners. These include our tendency to see the omnipresence of slaves in literary and legal texts "only through the veil of these slaveholding authors," where any number of distortions may have been applied to "meld slaves into objects or erase them from the scene altogether."[9] In the case of archaeological evidence, our modern preference still tends toward the spectacular "rooms with painted walls and mosaic floors, spaces associated with owners and the privileged" in contrast to non-descript "service areas like kitchens," workshops and agricultural outbuildings.[10] This tendency is rampant in contemporary Israeli archaeology, which privileges sites and projects that draw and awe tourists, and displaces the most compelling artifacts from their original context for display in air-conditioned museums.[11] Even industrial spaces, which frequently operated with enslaved activity, are interpreted for the "presence of equipment or the relevant technological processes but often seem to forget the workers."[12]

Patterson advocates for a "comparative method," which can fill the gaps created by missing evidence by analogizing from other slaveholding societies. This method is to be invoked last of all, when it is "the only recourse after having exhausted what we can learn by the available evidence."[13] Rome, Greece and Egypt are all societies from which comparisons might be taken, and I draw from scholarship of domestic architecture and

---

[9] Sandra R. Joshel and Lauren Hackworth Petersen, *The Material Life of Roman Slaves* (Cambridge, UK: Cambridge University Press, 2012), 5.
[10] Ibid.
[11] As was the case with late Roman synagogue mosaics from Khirbet Wadi Hammam, excavated by my field director Uzi Leibner, which now hang in the ticket corridor of the Israel Museum with only a small plaque describing their significance.
[12] Joshel and Petersen, 6.
[13] Patterson, 32.

funerary practices from other parts of the empire, as well as military and legal practices reflective of the *Pax Romana*.

My approach is to use evidence from around the Roman empire to shine new light on the primary evidence from first century Israel, which has not been thoroughly catalogued. Such a catalogue is necessary for several reasons. First, second temple historians and New Testament scholars frequently rely on evidence from outside the region to understand slavery and its influence on both the economic and thought worlds of the first century. Dale Martin's *Slavery as Salvation*, which relies on epigraphs and realia from around the empire, but not Palestine, is illustrative of this. By putting as much of the first century Palestinian materials together in one place, I hope to demonstrate that there is a large enough corpus for future scholarly engagement. Second, in specifically examining the archaeological materials, I hope to encourage reinterpretation of sites and contexts in light of the evidence for potential enslaved activities.

Any approach needs to take seriously the concerns laid out by Glancy, Joshel, Petersen and Patterson. For this reason, I have included only epigraphs that specifically reference enslaved status. This has meant the exclusion of some potentially fascinating, but inconclusive, connections between foreign names on ossuaries in family tombs and their potential to represent slave burials, as suggested by Samuel Klein.[14] In terms of archaeology, I have specifically chosen sites where the practice of slavery is attested in a literary source; doubtless slavery was practiced at other locations, elite or otherwise. When considering the literary canon, I have tried to focus on episodes where slavery is represented as a first century practice, not a rhetorical, literary or historical device. Thus I

---

[14] See Hezser, 50.

consider Herod's treatment of his household slaves in Josephus, while ignoring the numerous references to the Jews' first century political situation as 'slavery to the Romans,' and to the Israelites' former bondage in Egypt. In the New Testament, I consider individual enslaved persons who are part of the narrative, but not the use of slavery in parables or in figurative theological language. An examination of these is more appropriate to an exegetical or literary analysis than a historical one. Still, I have tried to show a general willingness to make connections where possible. In so doing, I hope to avoid explicitly re-inscribing the silences imposed by both the archaeological challenges in the region and the poor materiality of slavery itself.

State of Current Scholarship

Slavery has emerged as an important subject of study both for the Roman empire and the specific context of first century Palestine, and a number of works in recent years have addressed the subject. A variety of sociological and studies in the late seventies and early eighties laid the groundwork for modern approaches in the field. Keith Hopkins' 1978 *Conquerors and Slaves: Sociological Studies in Roman History,* for example, sees slavery as part of the cycle of continuous militarism that dominated the late Republican state, leading to a "scheme of interdependence"[15] that was unbreakable even as the economic and human toll became extreme. Sir Moses Finley's groundbreaking 1980 work, *Ancient Slavery and Modern Ideology*, was the first to formulate the idea of "slave societies," characterized by systemic political, economic and social dependence on slavery, as opposed to its incidental practice. In 1982 Orlando Patterson identified the philosophical and

---
[15] Hopkins, 12.

sociological elements common to the practice of slavery across times and places in his book *Slavery and Social Death*, a study in which ancient Greece and Rome factored heavily. This work was followed in 1987 by that of Keith Bradley, who examined the sociological and anthropological dimensions of Roman slavery specifically in his volume *Slaves and Masters in the Roman Empire: A Study in Social Control*. These early studies are in part responding to the Marxist view of slavery as a historical inevitability in the emergence of the western social system,[16] an approach that did not allow for comparisons between ancient and contemporary forms of slavery. By contrast the system articulated by Hopkins does not follow Marxist theory, and Finley specifically counters the views of the Mainz school and his Soviet contemporaries.[17] Patterson and Bradley make the specific case for a comparative approach, arguing that knowledge gained from slave systems in other periods of history can be employed to fill in gaps in the ancient record.

The need to respond to explicitly Marxist sociologies has declined in recent decades, even as more recent studies have continued the anthropological and sociological approach. These include Jean Andreau and Raymond Descat's *The Slave in Greece and Rome*, Enrico Dal Lago and Constantina Katsari's edited volume *Slave Systems Ancient and Modern*, Sandra Joshel's *Slavery in the Roman World* and, most recently, Peter Hunt's *Ancient Greek and Roman Slavery*. These works give consideration to the considerable developments in both critical theory and post-colonial thought that has emerged since the end of the twentieth century. As a consequence, they call attention to two important concepts that shape our understanding of ancient slavery. The first is the role that power systems, both

---

[16] Finley, "Ancient Slavery," 12ff.
[17] Ibid., 55-66.

ancient and modern, operate on our ways of understanding, our use of language and the relative importance we give to individual pieces of evidence. Second, see Roman slavery as part of a larger colonial enterprise, allowing further comparison to modern social systems.

Two volumes have sought to deal specifically with the archaeology of ancient slavery. Michele George's *Roman Slavery and Roman Material Culture* assembles essays from seven scholars that work principally with direct material evidence of slavery. Their primary sources range from graffiti and funerary epigraphy to artistic depictions of slavery in media such as statuary, engravings, wall paintings and mosaics. George's volume does not address the broader material world in which slaves lived, or offer methods for interpreting archaeological contexts in light of sociological knowledge about slavery. Sandra Joshel and Lauren Hackworth Petersen's 2011 work *The Material Lives of Roman Slaves* attempts to correct this problem, offering a variety of methods from contemporary cultural theorists that can aid in recovering previously overlooked evidence. An examination of the advantages and disadvantages of both George's and Joshel's and Petersen's approaches can be found in Chapter 2.

Slavery in Roman Palestine has also been the subject of a variety of recent studies by scholars of religious texts and traditions. Dale Martin, for example, draws heavily from epigraphy around the empire to illuminate the background of Paul's New Testament slavery discourses, identifying hundreds of family relations, occupations and examples of manumission in his 1990 book *Slavery as Salvation: The Metaphor of Slavery in Pauline Christianity*. Martin's work, while exhaustive when considering the Pauline materials and their Anatolian-Greek context, omits completely the situation of slavery in first century Palestine. Subsequent rhetorical studies of slavery in the New Testament include I.A.H.

Combes *The Metaphor of Slavery in the Writings of the Early Church* and John Byron's *Slavery Metaphors in Early Judaism and Pauline Christianity*. More recently, Albert Harrill's *Slaves in the New Testament* has attempted to offer a comprehensive analysis of all of the New Testament texts dealing with the subject, drawing in parallels from dozens of Greek and Roman writers and literary forms, though his work raises questions about the extent to which the authors of the New Testament were familiar with writings from other time periods and parts of the empire. Jennifer Glancy's *Slavery in Early Christianity* traces the subject diachronically from the New Testament period into the Christian writers of late antiquity. Glancy's first chapter on the life and sayings of Jesus is particularly helpful to this study as it identifies many of the relevant gospel passages related to slavery. The 2010 volume *Beyond Slavery: Overcoming its Religious and Sexual Legacies*, edited by Bernadette Brooten, attempts to examine hermeneutically how a variety of religious texts, including the Hebrew Bible, New Testament and subsequent Jewish, Christian and Muslim traditions have impacted historical and contemporary understandings of slavery.

Three further works address specifically the questions of Jewish practice and the Palestine in antiquity. Paul Flesher's *Oxen, Women or Citizens? Slaves in the System of the Mishnah* deals narrowly with references to slavery in the early rabbinic writings, highlighting the problems created by the ownership of rational, thinking persons and the extent to which enslaved persons free will was subordinated to the masters'. Catherine Hezser's more comprehensive *Jewish Slavery in Antiquity* compares the attitudes and practices of Hellenistic and Roman Jews to those of the broader empire, making use of archaeological and epigraphic evidence as well as the extensive literary record. I have attempted to include her analyses in cases where we deal with the same primary sources.

David Rokeah's 2012 book העבדות בעת העתיקה: בישראל, בנצרות הקדומה ובעולם היווני-הרומי (*Slavery in Antiquity: In Israel, in Early Christianity and in the Greco-Roman World*) compares slavery in Judaism, early Christianity and the rest of the empire, primarily through the identification of parallel literary and epigraphic sources.

Despite the excellent scholarship that has been done to date, there is still considerable room for additional work in the field. At present, none of these works presents a comprehensive catalogue of archaeological and literary evidence for slavery in Palestine during any period of antiquity. Hezser's work comes closest, but many of the important passages in Josephus, and does not consider epigraphs pertaining to non-Jewish persons. In addition, with the exception perhaps of Flesher, the specific context of first century Palestine is never treated on its own terms, despite the considerable cultural upheavals that delineate this time period from the century before, and especially after. By focusing specifically on the first century, it is possible to make clear how slavery as practiced in this period played a crucial role in maintaining the social and political apparatus of the late second temple period.

Chapter 2: Method

In this chapter I outline the methods that I will use to examine the epigraphic, archaeological and literary evidence in connection with each other. I begin by examining the methodological gaps identified by Michele George, gaps that arise out of both our incomplete knowledge of slavery as a social institution and the poor material record left behind by all marginalized persons in the ancient world, which leaves a bias toward elite contexts and concerns. I then explore the interdisciplinary approach of Ian Morris as a potential strategy for synthesizing data from archaeological and literary sources. I further consider the 're-imagining' strategies of Sandra Joshel and Lauren Hackworth Petersen, which apply modern critical theories to questions of archaeological visibility and bias. Finally, I resolve some challenges specific to an examination of first century Palestine, including questions of archaeological scarcity, political and geographic unity, and terminology.

The "Archaeology and History" Approach

In both her book chapter on "Slavery and Roman Material Culture" and the introduction to her own edited volume, *Roman Slavery and Roman Material Culture*, Michele George points to the twin challenges in identifying evidence for slavery in the archaeological record. First, there is the issue of poor materiality: according to George, "the poor quality of housing, clothing and other goods used by slaves that reduces their chances of survival in the archaeological record and makes it impossible to reconstruct, for example, slave religion, diet, or other aspects of a slave subculture."[18] This is true even in environments with exceptional material remains such as Ostia or Pompeii; the problem is even more substantial in archaeological landscapes with poor preservation, pervasive subsequent reoccupation, or sociopolitical challenges to extensive excavation. As I have described above, all of these concerns are present in the archaeology of Palestine. This problem worsens when an excessive burden of proof is subjected to the connection between slavery and a particular material object or context. Even at sites where there is exceptional epigraphic or literary evidence for slavery, there is some hesitancy to ascribe slave identity or activity to particular objects.

This hesitance may be in part due to a bias in favor of elite objects, spaces and concerns in the practice of archaeology and art history in general. George writes, that art historians (and I believe, scholars in general), "have tended to put issues of greatest importance to the Roman elite, such as style, chronology, imperial influence or political motivation, ahead of those germane to lower-status groups."[19] Such a bias may be natural for several reasons. First, the literary works that figure so prominently in the study of the ancient past were almost always the product of social elites; as a consequence the 'voices' of the past that still speak to us, speak of elite concerns. Scholars themselves may also more comfortably self-identify with the Roman ruling class than with a social group, such as enslaved persons, whose situation and concerns are almost completely unknown to us. Perhaps most importantly, though, our own aesthetic and enthusiasm is drawn toward the

---

[18] Michele George, ed., *Roman Slavery and Roman Material Culture* (Toronto: University of Toronto Press, 2013), 385.
[19] Ibid.

most grand and spectacular of ancient remains: palaces, temples and triumphal monuments, even if they did not represent life for most ordinary persons. These places are not, by and large, seen as slave spaces.[20]

Acknowledging these limitations by speaking for the necessity of accounting for slavery as "a fundamental social institution with multiple implications for Roman society,"[21] identifies a variety of archaeological and art history subjects requiring further scholarly inquiry. These include slave quarters within the domestic context, evidence for the slave trade and captives, and slavery in funerary contexts, as well as artistic depictions of domestic service, scenes of military captives, and illustrations of industrial activities traditionally performed by slaves.[22]

To this list I would add epigraphy and papyrology, which, though they are less strictly archaeological and art historical, are generally accessed through archaeological methods and describe particular sites and social contexts. Still, George's methods do not take the 'next step' from, for example, 'illustrations of industrial activities,' to reasoning about the people that performed them when evidence of those activities is discovered in the archaeological landscape. For the slavery researcher, each such find raises an important question: given the connection between, say, flour milling and enslaved labor, is the presence of a flour mill in the archaeological record evidence of slavery? George's approach is particularly helpful when considering objects that offer rich evidence of slavery, such as the milling scene from Pompeii illustrated in Figure 12. On the other hands,

---

[20] The Roman Colosseum is perhaps one exception, as the connection between slavery, gladiatorial violence, and capital punishment becomes more widely known.
[21] George, 1.
[22] George, 386-411.

gaps in the archaeological record or uncertainty about the interpretation of individual objects may lead to important omissions. Other methods, like the "Interdisciplinary Approach" and "Re-Imagining Approach," described below, offer strategies for filling in the gaps between specific objects and illustrations to provide a more comprehensive picture of ancient slavery.

The "Interdisciplinary" Approach

In attempting to frame the challenges for archaeology of enslaved populations in classical Athens, Ian Morris argues for a more interdisciplinary approach that makes use of all of the available resources about slavery, including legal and literary texts together with material remains. Morris is writing in response to the challenges put forward by Moses Finley and Walter Scheidel. Finley had had argued that archaeology alone was not sufficient to uncover the complex "legal and economic" structures that underlay the Roman slave system; Scheidel that "it is unreasonable to expect archaeology to make a significant contribution to modern reconstructions of the Greek or Roman slave-systems."[23] Morris responds that, while both Finley and Scheidel have identified a potentially significant problem, the conclusion that there will "never be an archaeology of ancient slavery," as Scheidel suggests, is overstated. Instead, archaeologists must be willing to engage in "a sustained attack on methodological problems"[24] and a new willingness to engage directly with emerging archeo-science and the evidence of classical texts.

---

[23] Scheidel, 581; Quoted in Morris, 176.
[24] Ibid., 193.

To begin with, Morris points to advances in the applications of forensic anthropology, and specifically detailed analyses of skeletal remains to identify diet and living conditions.[25] Previously it was possible only in general terms to determine the health of an individual through ancient skeletal remains; now "systematic comparisons of, the relative nutrition, health, joint wear, age at death, and sex ratios of the free and slave populations" and even DNA relationships can be brought to bear, provided that distinct populations can be identified reliably.[26] The presence of a single female skeletal forearm in the ruins of the Burnt House, for example, raises questions of the victim's identity. Was she a household slave or a member of the priestly family? Modern population genetics and isotope analyses, not possible at the time of Avigad's 1967 discovery, might answer questions like that more definitively in future finds. The challenge, according to Morris, lies in securing reliable archaeological markers that can be used to make distinctions between enslaved and non-enslaved persons. The same is true, I would argue, of contexts such as slave quarters and objects of daily life.

One way to develop archaeological markers is to rely on textual evidence that is already suggestive of slave locations, activities or practices within a specific geographic context. It is true that Mediterranean archaeology has a complex relationship with texts, in part due to the excesses of 19th century Greek and biblical archaeologists, as well as to the historical criticism that has been applied to texts more recently. Still, Morris is willing to draw elementary conclusions from literary sources, and use them as a starting point. In the case of his analysis of cemeteries near the famous source of Attic silver, Laurium, he

---

[25] Ibid.
[26] Ibid., 178.

concludes that we can have "some confidence in assuming that some areas (like the classical Lavreotiki) had high densities of slaves provides one starting point."[27] The basis for this confidence is the reported Spartan defection of slaves described in Thucydides 7.27, who writes, "more than twenty thousand slaves had deserted, a great part of them artisans," καὶ ἀνδραπόδων πλέον ἢ δύο μυριάδες ηὐτομολήκεσαν, καὶ τούτων τὸ πολὺ μέρος χειροτέχναι.

    Morris does not offer explicit methods for evaluating the usefulness of ancient texts in the archaeological project. Still, his example can, I believe, be used to construct minimum criteria from which it is safe to apply texts to an interdisciplinary approach to an archaeology of slavery. First, Morris is working in a locale, time period and context where there is high confidence for the presence of slaves. There is little scholarly debate that classical Athens was a slaveholding society, or that mining was an activity carried out by enslaved populations. If material evidence of slavery were to be found *anywhere* in classical Attica, Laurium would be one of the best places to look for it. Second, there is the question of genre. The passage in question takes both a factual and ambivalent approach to this slavery. Thucydides 7 is not a metaphor, a parable or a philosophical maxim: it is part of a historical narrative about a military conflict for which there is ample literary and material evidence. Finally, slavery at Laurium is described with a scale and specificity that, if factually reported, should leave some mark on the archaeological landscape. The presence of *twenty thousand* enslaved persons at work in the mines (or even two thousand, granting Thucydides the liberty of a tenfold exaggeration) would undoubtedly be accompanied by ample material remains.

---

[27] Ibid., 193

Confidence that a significant portion of the population of the Laverotiki cemetery were enslaved allows us to reconsider the objectives of archaeology with respect to ancient slavery. Morris argues that scholars should not be content with seeking out evidence for "slavery's economic and social structures," but to try "to re-experience slaves' lives through the immediacy of physical remains."[28] Undoubtedly, this approach offers an important strategy for recovering the historical realities of life for persons marginalized by the legal and social stigmas of slavery. Still, Morris suggests caution, warning against "lowering the bar on conventional scholarly standards of falsification."[29]

In this project, I rely on Morris' strategy of using texts to develop archaeological markers that identify slave contexts. My own rules have been formulated as follows. First, a text must explicitly refer to slavery as practiced in first century Palestine. Rhetorical, metaphorical or theological uses are excluded. Thus Jesus' parable of the wicked tenants (Luke 20:9-19) and Josephus' frequent references to the Jews' preference for death over slavery are omitted: even if they are useful for understanding the thought world of first century Palestinian slavery, they cannot help in the identification of archaeological contexts. Second, I have preferred texts and contexts where the practice of slavery is consistent with broader Roman practice. In selecting a reading of an ossuary as indicative of an enslaved physician, for example, I note the presence of this practice in other parts of the empire. Finally, I have presumed the presence of certain commonplace slave activities on the basis of less common ones. Thus in the Herodian palaces, I have assumed that enslaved persons were involved in domestic and banqueting activity, due to the literary

---

[28] Ibid., 188-189.
[29] Ibid.

evidence for enslaved and formerly enslaved estate managers and royal attendants. This is admittedly less certain; nonetheless it is difficult to imagine a situation in which enslaved persons ran the estate and free persons washed the dishes.

On this basis, as in the example of Laurium, we can have some confidence that slavery occurred in specific locales in first century Palestine on the basis of textual evidence. These include, as outlined below, the elite housing in the Jewish Quarter of Jerusalem, Herodian royal estates, and locations in Galilee identified in New Testament and Mishnaic sources. In addition, the discovery of epigraphic evidence, another category of 'text' to be reconciled, adds Yavneh and Khirbet Qumran as starting points for interdisciplinary investigation of slavery.

The "Re-Imagining" Approach

Making the leap from gathering artifacts of ancient slavery to reconstructing the material and thought worlds of enslaved persons requires a methodological approach that overcomes biases both ancient and modern. Sandra Joshel and Lauren Hackworth Petersen attempt to offer such an approach in the introduction to their book *The Material Life of Roman Slaves*. Following the model of theorist Michel de Certeau,[30] they organize activities in the material landscape into *strategies*, which enable slaveholders to perpetuate enslavement and maximize the use of enslaved bodies and actions for their own benefit, and *tactics*, which allow enslaved persons to interact with the physical landscape in ways that foster resistance to their subjugation. Both strategies and tactics have an intimate

---

[30] Joshel and Petersen, 8-9.

connection to place: strategies occur in "a place that can be delimited as its *own*,"[31] a space controlled by slaveholders and their allies, including the local and imperial governments. Tactics, on the other hand, "must play on and with terrain imposed on it."[32]

In both a legal and physical sense, slaveholders controlled most or all of the physical environment in which slaves operated. This control extended not only to places, including "house, villa, farm, workshop, baths and mill"[33] but to objects as well: within contexts where slavery occurred, every physical object not only served the utility of the slaveholder, but enhanced his or her status as well, a status gained and maintained through the exploitation of enslaved labor. Control of physical spaces also extended to *movement*; Roman slavery "included various practices for controlling slave mobility."[34] By taking this broader view, Joshel and Petersen are able to see how a whole range of spaces and artifacts discoverable by archaeology can inform our knowledge of Roman slavery.

The "master's view," as Joshel and Petersen describe it, is only half the story, however. They offer three approaches for interpreting enslaved activity within a landscape and object space controlled by masters. The first is to re-imagine the ways in which "the slave owner's space might be put to other uses by the slave."[35] These uses include various respites from work and supervision. Second, they pay special attention to "areas like kitchens, stable yards and back doors" which, though owned by the master, were yielded to slave activity and control "out of the gaze of owners."[36] Finally, they interpret enslaved movement "in three dimensions," focusing on the "complex temporal and spatial

---

[31] Ibid.
[32] Ibid.
[33] Ibid., 9
[34] Ibid., 10
[35] Ibid., 16
[36] Ibid., 17

calculations" slaves might employ in support of their tactics, a category of data they find entirely lacking in the literary record.[37]

Joshel and Petersen's approach acknowledges that, in the Roman practice of slavery, almost every material context implicated slaveowner strategy and slaveholder tactics. As such, simple cataloguing of slavery-related artifacts will likely omit important information about the material life of enslaved persons. Instead, public and private spaces must be interrogated with knowledge gained from the literary record and cross-cultural understanding.

There are limits to such an approach, however. Joshel and Petersen work primarily with materials from first century Italy, and benefit from the spectacular, and accidental, preservation of sites like Pompeii, Herculaneum and Ostia Antiqua.

Complex analyses of the visual and spatial environment are possible, in part, because that visual and spatial environment still exists for our modern eyes to examine. In Israel, preservation is much more uneven, requiring considerable speculation. Still, a few sites are well-defined enough to undertake their kind of analysis. In order to avoid over-applying this approach in historically uncertain environments, I have limited my examinations to specific archaeological contexts where there the extant literary and epigraphic record suggests a high likelihood of enslaved activity. For this reason, I feel confident in reading enslaved activity at the site of milling installation in Capernaum, a community that included enslaved persons according to pericopes found in multiple gospel traditions. Likewise I interpret service areas of the Burnt House and Mansion house in Jersualem's Jewish Quarter as slave spaces, since Josephus, the New Testament and Jewish

---

[37] Ibid.

traditions all speak of the houses' owners as slaveholders. Beginning with non-archaeological evidence for slaveholding in these contexts allows for an exploration of the physical spaces that shed light on enslaved activities and experiences in first century Palestine.

Challenges with Archaeology in the Region

Uncovering the realia of slavery in Roman Palestine requires attentiveness to the specific archaeological challenges of the region, which derive both from its unique geography and population history, as well as its politics in the last hundred years. In the introduction to his 1978 book *The Archaeology of the Land of Israel*, Yohanan Aharoni writes that "there are three features which determine the general character of Eretz-Israel: it is small, greatly fragmented and poor in natural resources."[38] Israel is, according to Aharoni, only "12 percent of the area of Italy or 30 percent of the area of Greece."[39] The comparatively small size of the region has certain advantages: travel within the country is straightforward (including, albeit with certain challenges, the Palestinian territories of the West Bank) and both Israeli and foreign archaeologists are familiar with most of the major sites and their similarities and differences from one another. The country's fragmentation, on the other hand, is more problematic for archaeologists. Israel is a country of boundaries: physical as well as political. Its coastal plain gives way to steep mountain terrain only a few miles inland, and varies in elevation from over 1000 meters in some parts of the country to more than 200 meters below sea level in the volcanic rift from

---

[38] Yohanan Aharoni and Miriam Aharoni, The Archaeology of the Land of Israel: From the Prehistoric Beginnings to the End of the First Temple Period (Philadelphia: Westminster Press, 1982), 1.
[39] Ibid.

which the Jordan valley and Dead Sea are formed. As a result, "the sharp topographical contrasts fragment the country into quite different climatic zones in spite of geographical proximity,"[40] a fact that, according to Aharoni, "has always encouraged division into separate ethnic units."[41] We should expect the materiality of slavery, especially in its agricultural form, to be highly dependent on the modes of food production and the cultural strategies it engenders; while these factors differ regionally in other parts of the Mediterranean, contrasts are much more localized in Israel. This fact is exaggerated by the relative poverty of natural resources found in the country. The Italian pattern of extensive farming estates employing enslaved workers would not be possible in most of the country. The entire region is extremely dry, and "drought years are regular phenomena during which precipitation is inadequate in most of the land."[42] A few valleys can support agriculture, as can hilltop sites aided by terracing and complex irrigation. Much of the remaining territory is "too arid to permit systematic agriculture."[43]

This potential for cultural disunity caused Roger Moorey, in his book *Excavation in Palestine*, to propose two questions that are essential to the evaluation of sites and material contexts from Israel, even when dealing with an extensive historical record. The first is whether "the archaeological record [contains] homogeneous groups of objects (or cultures) which may in practice be distinguished from other groups."[44] In the context of slavery, this question cuts two ways. With limited evidence, it may be impossible to distinguish materials unique to the practice of slavery from the broader cultural context. More

---

[40] Ibid., 2
[41] Ibid., 3
[42] Ibid., 4
[43] Ibid., 5
[44] P. R. S. Moorey, *Excavation in Palestine (Cities of the Biblical World)* (Guildford, Surrey: Lutterworth Press, 1981), 16

significantly, though, the interpreter may encounter multiple cultural groups within a small geographic area, each with their own unique practices and material habits. Moorey's second question, whether specific objects are in fact, "really the material expression of a social group or people,"[45] is a theoretical one, but one where texts, historical or otherwise, can provide significant additional evidence. Archaeology is a messy business, and determining the dating and context of objects can be problematic. This is especially problematic for Jerusalem, which underwent a dramatic destruction during the period of our study followed by a rebuilding and population replacement at the beginning of the second century. The rich literary evidence from the period can in many cases constitute an "independent historical framework,"[46] but one that is fraught with challenges.

Some of these challenges arise out of the fact that many of the texts in question form the central religious and ethical corpora for two of the world's major religions. This connection matters for modern identity politics in the region. As Katharina Galor points out, "the claims that modern Israeli citizens are descendants of the Israelites or Hasmoneans and that the early Christians and Muslims of the region were the ancestors of today's Palestinian Christians and Muslims, respectively, are only rarely challenged."[47] Connection to the biblical tradition was also the original impetus for archaeology of the Holy Land. As critical approaches to biblical scholarship evolved during the nineteenth century, scholars on both sides looked to archaeology to answer questions about the text. Tomis Kapitan writes, "Protestant Christians were particularly concerned to deflect

---

[45] Ibid.
[46] Ibid.
[47] Katharina Galor and Gideon Avni, Unearthing Jerusalem 150 Years of Archaeological Research in the Holy City (Warsaw, Ind.: Eisenbrauns, 2011), 2.

criticism of the bible by seeking archaeological support for the historicity of biblical accounts."[48] This impetus to "confirm the bible" through excavation and interpretation is still present in the field in a number of ways.

As Kapitan points out, Jewish religious and political ideology also factor significantly in Israeli archaeology. He writes that, "in the past 50 years… the work of Israeli archaeologists [has] aimed at deepening the connection between Jews and what they regard as the ancient Jewish homeland."[49] In some cases, modern day Jewish claims to the land have been formulated through the lens of a homogeneous and uniquely Jewish presence in antiquity. This has led to accusations that the contemporary practice of archaeology in Israel actively undermines links between the material record and the modern Palestinian community. Some scholars, most notably the late American Albert Glock, have attempted to counter this tendency by attempting "to link the contemporary Palestinian Arab community with the archaeological remains found in Palestine."[50] Ultimately, as Yaacov Shavit points, out, "no group in Israel has a monopoly on the historical knowledge divulged by archaeology."

Geographic Terminology

In such a politically charged context, even the names used to describe the region can become problematic. The area comprising the modern day state of Israel and the Palestinian territories was not a political unity in the first century: it comprised all or part

---

[48] Albert E. Glock and Tomis Kapitan, Archaeology, History, and Culture in Palestine and the Near East : Essays in Memory of Albert E. Glock (Atlanta, Ga.: Scholars Press, 1999), ix.
[49] Kapitan, ix.
[50] Kapitan, x

of regions then known as Judea, Samaria, Philistia, Galilee, Idumea, Gaulanitis and the Decapolis. The name Israel continued to be associated with the region due to traditions about its prior political unity in the Iron Age, which factored significantly in the religious and political ideologies of the Jews described in the Hebrew Bible and Josephus. Greeks, since Herodotus, called the region Palestine. In his 1999 paper "Palestine and Israel," David Jacobson traces the history of the term "Palestine" and its use in referring to the entirety of the region. He writes, "Although some of Herodotus' references to Palestine are compatible with a narrow definition of the coastal strip of the Land of Israel, it is clear that Herodotus does call the whole land by the name of the coastal strip."[51] This usage continues, according to Jacobson, in the writings of Aristotle, Ovid, Statius and Dio Chrysostom. Ovid, for instance, refers to the Jewish sabbath as a festival kept by "the Syrians of Palestine."[52] Chrysostom likewise locates the Dead Sea in the "interior of Palestine."[53] Philo, in is *Life of Moses*, calls the region into which Moses led the Jewish people in the Exodus "Palestine."[54] Josephus writes in of *Antiquities* 1.6.4 that "Trachonitis and Damascus" are "situated between Palestine and Coele Syria,"[55] suggesting that the broader definition of Palestine included Galilee. His usage here contrasts with his own narrower use of the term only two paragraphs earlier (1.6.2), in which he says that the Greeks call Palestine the "region between Egypt and Gaza." In his paper "Flavius Josephus and His Portrayal of the Coast (Paralia) of Contemporary Roman Palestine: Geography and Ideology," the Israeli scholar Ben-Zion Rosenfeld suggests that the real distinction is ideological and theological for

---

[51] David M. Jacobson, "Palestine and Israel." BASOR, no. 313 (1999): 65.
[52] Ovid, *Art of Love* 1.416. Cf. Jacobson, 66.
[53] Jacobson, 66
[54] Philo, *Life of Moses*, 163. Cf. Jacobson, 66.
[55] *AJ* 1.6.4. Cf. Jacobson, 66.

Josephus; thus while Judea "sometimes conforms with the biblical utopian vision encompassing all the territory allocated to the Jews-Eretz Israel-and sometimes refers only to a part," for Rosenfeld Palestine "signifies the whole region connected with the land of Israel in Josephus' time."[56] I follow the same convention here, deferring to ancient use without untangling the conflicting claims over modern uses of the term.

---

[56] Ben-Zion Rosenfeld, "Flavius Josephus and His Portrayal of the Coast (Paralia) of Contemporary Roman Palestine: Geography and Ideology." *The Jewish Quarterly Review* 91, no. 1/2 (2000): 145.

Chapter 3: Epigraphic Evidence

Uncovering evidence of slavery in the epigraphy of first century Palestine poses several challenges. First, a variety of languages and writing systems were in use throughout the period. Classical Hebrew, essentially extinct as a spoken language in the first century, continued as the language of prayer, sacred texts and religious discourse. Its sister language Aramaic was the local language of daily life. The writing system for both languages was in active transition from the earlier 'Canaanite' form to the one we know today during the late Hellenistic and early Roman period. Greek had become the lingua franca in the eastern Empire during the conquests of Alexander, and a first language for many foreigners living in the land, as well as in the cities earlier founded by Greek colonists and mercenaries, including those of the Decapolis and coastal plain. Latin was spoken by the Roman governors and entourage, large contingents of occupying soldiers, and transplants from the western Empire, especially at Caesarea.

While there are many well preserved sites, there are no equivalents to Pompeii, Herculaneum, Ostia Antiqua or Ephesus in Israel. Neither was the country home to any major international metropolis like Rome, Athens or Alexandria. As a consequence, the epigraphic record is much thinner. At present, the four published volumes of the *Corpus Inscriptionum Iudaeae/Palistinae* contain about 4,500 inscriptions in total. Still, slavery has left its written mark on the material landscape, principally through funerary inscriptions, as well as a single commercial document.

Five inscriptions are presented here, all from the first century CE: two from Jerusalem, two from Jericho and surroundings, and one from the countryside near Yavneh. Each illustrates a distinctive aspect of slave practice in early Roman Palestine. The first, JERU0050, corresponds to the ossuary of an enslaved physician. The second relates the name of a freed slave of the imperial household. The third demonstrates the practice of freeing and then marrying an enslaved woman, in this instance, probably a former war captive. The fourth inscription attests to the use of formerly enslaved persons as estate managers and overseers, a practice which may shed light on several passages and characters from both the gospels and Josephus. The final inscription, from Qumran, raises questions about the intersection between slavery and the sectarian religious communities of the first century.

JERU0050: The "Captive Physician"

Diplomatic Form	Not available.
Transcription	תרפט הנשבה (*trpṭ hnšbh*)
Translation	the captive physician
Description and Source	Upon an ossuary found at Abu Tor, Jerusalem. *Catalogue of Jewish Ossuaries*, 97.[57]

This ossuary inscription, found at Abu Tor, Jerusalem, is documented as item 80 in L.

---

[57] See entry for JERU0050 in the Inscriptions of Israel/Palestine Catalogue (Brown University). Online at https://library.brown.edu/cds/projects/iip/viewinscr/jeru0050/. Accessed 1/14/19.

Y. Rahmani's *Catalogue of Jewish Ossuaries.*[58] The ossuary dates to the late Second Temple period, from about 20 BCE to 70 CE. The text, in Aramaic, reads "תרפט הנשבה" (*trpṭ hnšbh*), for which Rahmani offers several possible interpretations which pertain to slavery. He suggests that the plain Aramaic meaning of *trpṭ,* 'lax,' makes no sense, and that a transliteration of a Greek word is favored. One possibility he puts forward is θρεπτος, a word commonly used to mean a "slave, bred in the house."[59] This interpretation is at odds, however, with the adjective *nšbh,* which suggests a captive or oppressed person: house born slaves are, by definition, neither captured nor impressed into slavery. Instead, Rahmani's preferred reading is a form of θεραπευτης, a word that can mean "servant, caretaker or worshipper, but also medical attendant."[60] There is, according to Rahmani, extensive use of the word with the latter meaning in Jewish and Christian literature of the time, and the term is used as with an occupational meaning in at least two other Semitic inscriptions. As a consequence, his preferred translation is "the captive physician."

Second Temple ossuaries from Jerusalem rarely contain inscriptions other than the name and familial associations of the deceased and occasional religious or moralizing epitaphs. As a consequence, this find, in which only the deceased's occupation and servile status are recorded, is somewhat unusual. The employment of enslaved physicians, especially in elite households during the early Roman period, is however well-documented in other parts of the empire. C. A. Forbes, in his essay, "The Education and Training of Slaves in Antiquity," identifies literary, historical and epigraphic instances for enslaved,

---

[58] L. Y. Rahmani, Rashut Ha-'atiḳot Israel, and Muze'on Yiśra'el, *A Catalogue of Jewish Ossuaries in the Collections of the State of Israel.* (Jerusalem: Israel Antiquities Authority, The Israel Academy of Sciences and Humanities, 1994), 97.
[59] Ibid.
[60] Ibid.

domestic physicians throughout the empire, beginning in the early Imperial period, many of whom, he suggests, possessed considerable education and skill. These included not only slaves of the imperial household, such as the anonymous physician of Augustus described in Suetonius' *Caligula* 8.4,[61] but among members of the senatorial class, such as Apuleius' medical slave Themison, mentioned in Book 33 of his *Apologia*.[62][63]

The existence of JERU0050 offers us several insights into the practice of slavery during the period before the Jewish War. First, slavery was not confined to agricultural work or other forms of unskilled and undifferentiated labor; in at least this instance, enslaved persons performed skilled activities in which they might compete economically with free persons. Second, the simple fact of an ossuary burial for this enslaved person raises interesting questions about the funerary practices of slaveholding households in Judea and Jerusalem. These families purchased ossuaries for, and engaged in the distinctive secondary burial practices on behalf of, not only true 'blood' members of the household, but for enslaved occupants as well, a fact which raises interesting questions for current interpretations of ossuary epigraphy. Might many more of the thousands of ossuaries so far found have in fact contained the remains of enslaved persons?

JERI0007: Queen Agrippina's Freedman

Diplomatic Form	Not available.

---

[61] Clarence A. Forbes, "The Education and Training of Slaves in Antiquity." *Transactions and Proceedings of the American Philological Association* 86 (1955): 326.
[62] Ibid., 353.
[63] In later antiquity, there were even discourses about the benefits of enslaved physicians over hired ones, with Julian (7.207d) acknowledging the "ticklish situation of being obliged simultaneously to flatter and cure his master,"[63] an early and tacit recognition of subaltern tactics.

Transcription	Θεοδότου ἀπελευθέρου βασιλίσσης Ἀγριππείνης σορός
Translation	The ossuary of Theodotus the freedperson of Queen Agrippina
Description and Source	Upon an ossuary found at Tomb 8, Jericho. *Catalogue of Jewish Ossuaries*, 238-9.[64]

This ossuary, also from pre-revolt Judea, was found in Tomb H at Jericho.[65] The inscription reads Θεοδότου ἀπελευθέρου βασιλίσσης Ἀγριππείνης σορός, "the ossuary of Theodotos, the freed person of the Queen Agrippina." Rachel Hachlili, who first described the find, associates it with "Agrippina the Younger (15-59 CE) whose freedman, Theodotos, probably lived for some time in Rome but was buried in what was likely his family tomb at Jericho."[66] Catherine Hezser, in her investigation of the phenomenon of Jewish freedmen returning to Israel, concurs with this assessment.[67] Since Agrippina was murdered by her son Nero at least ten years before the onset of the Jewish war, Theodotos must have been taken into slavery through some previous military conquest, perhaps the early first century tax revolts. Alternately, he may have been born into an enslaved Jewish family at Rome, and reached Jericho through different circumstances; it is impossible to know.

Keith Hopkins writes, "The slave and ex-slaves of the emperor formed an especially privileged and powerful group. The status and power of their master rubbed off on them. Unlike nobles, ... they had time to accumulate power."[68] Added to this power might be a

---

[64] See entry for JERI0007 in the Inscriptions of Israel/Palestine Catalogue (Brown University). Online at https://library.brown.edu/cds/projects/iip/viewinscr/jeri0007/. Accessed 1/14/19.
[65] Rahmani, 238-239.
[66] Rachel Hachlili, "The Goliath Family in Jericho: Funerary Inscriptions from a First-Century A.D. Jewish Monumental Tomb." *Bulletin of the American Schools of Oriental Research* 235, no. Summer (1979): 31–65.
[67] Hezser, 50.
[68] Hopkins, 124.

peculium, money and property technically in the possession of the master but designated for the enslaved person's use, of considerable size. It is possible that Theodotus acquired considerable wealth and status due to his former servitude in the imperial household.

CIIP I.1 734: The Centurion and His Heiress

Diplomatic Form	T CL TI F POP FATALIS ROMA C LEG II AUG LEG X VIC LEG II AUG LEG XI C P F LEG XIV G M V LEG XII FUL LEG X FR III HAST VIX AN XLII MIL ANN XXIII CL IONICE LIB ET HERES OB ME RITA EIUS O T B Q
Transcription	Ti(berius) Cl(audius) Ti(beri) f(ilius) Pop(lilia) Fatalis | (domo) Roma C leg(ionis) II Aug(ustae), leg(ionis) XX | Vic(tricis), leg(ionis) II Aug(ustae), leg(ionis) XI C(laudiae) p(iae) f(idelis), | leg(ionis) XIV G(eminae) M(artiae) V(ictricis), leg(ionis) XII Ful(minatae), | leg(ionis) X Fr(etensis), III hast(atus) vix(it) an(nos) | XLII, mil(itavit) ann(os) XXIII. Cl(audia) | Ionice lib(erta) et heres ob me- | rita eius. O(ssa) t(ibi) b(ene) q(uiescant). T(erra) t(ibi) l(evis) s(it).
Translation	Tiberius Claudius Fatalis, son of Tiberius, of the tribe Poplilia, born in Rome. He was centurion in *legio II Augusta*, in *legio XX Victrix*, in *legio II Augusta*, in *legio XI Claudia*, the pious and trustworthy, in *legio XIV Gemina Martia Victrix*, in *legio XII Fulminata*, in *legio X Fretensis*, where he had the rank of a *tertius hastatus*. He lived 42 years and served in the army for 23 years. Claudia Ionice, his freedwoman and heiress erected this tomb on account of his merits. May your bones rest quietly, may the earth be light upon you.
Description and Source	Tablet in secondary use in Jerusalem. CIIP I.1.734.[69]

---

[69] See also *Database of Military Inscriptions and Papyri of Early Roman Palestine*, number 53. Online at https://armyofromanpalestine.com/0053-2. Accessed 1/14/19.

This highly abbreviated inscription of the Roman style memorializes Tiberius Claudius Fatalis, centurion of the third cohort of the tenth legion and catalogues his extensive military service. Historical knowledge of the presence of his legion at Jerusalem dates his death to the period between the Jewish War and Bar Kokhba revolt.[70] The tablet was found in secondary use as a drain cover inset in the city wall between the Damascus Gate and Herod's Gate in the Muslim Quarter of the city. The inscription is given in memory of him by "Claudia Ionice, lib(erta) et heres," his freedwoman and heiress.

On Roman epitaphs, a variety of terms are used to describe men's relationships with enslaved and formerly enslaved women. In his chapter on "Sex and Family Life," Peter Hunt describes the legal effects of Roman marriage law on the applicability of specific marriage terms to funerary epigraphy. He writes, "Roman law did not acknowledge the marriages or families of slaves. A male and female slave could only contract *contubernium*, informal marriage, and never an official marriage."[71] As a consequence, the term *contubernales*, literally 'tentmates,' is a frequent way in which freedwomen (and occasionally freedmen) describe their relationships with their late spouses. The term *contubernalis* presents challenges in the context of military epitaphs, and especially those who die away from home as did our Tiberius. Frequently, fellow soldiers will also use the term *contubernales* when erecting a monument for a deceased comrade. So while Claudia Ionice does not describe her relationship to her deceased partner using the most common term for marriages involving enslaved status, we cannot read much into that fact. The terms she used instead are intriguing: she is both *liberta* (freedwoman) and *heres* (heiress).

---

[70] Leah Di Segni and Werner Eck, eds. *Corpus Inscriptionum Iudaeae Palaestinae, Jerusalem Part 2* (Leiden: DeGruyter, 2018), 37-8.
[71] Peter Hunt, *Ancient Greek and Roman Slavery* (Hoboken, N.J.: John Wiley and Sons, 2017), 112.

They do not necessarily imply a romantic relationship: she may in fact be only a former slave of his household and his only living heir. It is more likely, however, that she was formerly his concubine, purchased for that purpose or acquired as a war prize during his years in service of the empire. She may have been freed only upon his death, specifically to inherit his estate.

Several scholars have attempted to shed light on the status of enslaved women in Roman Palestine. Tal Ilan covers such diverse topics as enslaved marriage in the Herodian family,[72] the impacts of various Greek philosophers on gendered slave relations[73] and the wisdom of rabbinic maidservants in the Talmudic tradition[74]. Cynthia Baker examines, among other things, the interconnection between women and slaves in the Rabbinic rules for the marketplace.[75] Catherine Hezser deals extensively with the phenomenon of concubinage as it is expressed in biblical law as well as the distinctions between 'Canaanite' and 'Hebrew' slaves.[76] The former is a term extended to encompass all Gentiles, including the centurion's widow. In these discourses, Jewish concerns dominate, especially when the rabbinic sources factor prominently in our understanding of gender relationships in the period. Comparatively little has been said, however, about women enslaved to non-Jewish households in Roman Palestine, since, according to Joshel and Petersen, "modern historians often repeat the silences of sources and archives."[77]

In her essay examining "Slaves and *Liberti* in the Roman Army" through the lens of a

---

[72] Tal Ilan, Integrating Women into Second Temple History (Texte Und Studien Zum Antiken Judentum, 76) (Tübingen: Mohr Siebeck, 1999), 23.
[73] Ibid., 129
[74] Ibid., 184-185.
[75] Cynthia M. Baker, *Rebuilding the House of Israel : Architectures of Gender in Jewish Antiquity*. (Stanford, Calif.: Stanford University Press, 2002), 83-89.
[76] Hezser 92-93, 189-193.
[77] Joshel and Petersen, 5.

stela from Germany dated to 9-10 CE, Natalie Boymel Kampen examines the place of enslaved individuals and free persons in the legions of Roman and foreign soldiers constantly-moving throughout the empire. She writes, "slaves and *liberti* were present in the military camps in a variety of roles, some of which created a degree of intimacy between them and their masters or patrons. They might be grooms and baggage handlers, fire strokers and craftsmen, personal servants or even children's attendants."[78] Undoubtedly, Roman soldiers might develop complex relationships, including romantic ones, with enslaved persons around the camp. Nonetheless, the special setting of foreign military expeditions actually amplified the power imbalance between slave and master in a number of ways. First, as Joseph Miller points out, the use of slaves "represented the strategy by which military elites, in contexts where they were marginal to a predominantly rural and communal ethos," were able to exercise power and control while immunizing themselves against local resistance.[79] Dependence on enslaved labor enabled, to some extent, independence from labor from local free persons who might organize to threaten military authority. In addition, the long distances and limited controls imposed on foreign legions meant there were little to no consequences, even socially, for abuse. No doubt, the enslaved wives of military personnel, neither free with the Roman system nor part of the local social order, were presented with serious challenges in navigating the social landscape.

CIIP III 2268: The Procurator's Wife

---

[78] Natalie Boymel Kampen, "Slaves and Liberti in the Roman Army." In George, 181.
[79] Joseph Miller, "Slavery as Historical Process: Examples from the Ancient Mediterranean and the Modern Atlantic," in Dal Lago and Katsari, 74.

Diplomatic Form	IULIA GRATA TI IULII AUG L MELLONTIS PROC
Transcription	Iulia Grata Ti(berius) Iulii Aug(ustus) L(ibertus) Mellontis Proc(urator)
Translation	Iulia Grata (wife) of Tiberius Iulius Augustus Libertus Mellontis, Procurator
Description and Source	Tablet found in orange grove near Yavneh. CIIP III.2268.

This inscription, found in an orange grove near Yavneh and dated to the early first century CE, further highlights the presence of freedmen and freedwomen of the Imperial household and the role that they had in the daily administration of Roman Palestine. It reads, "Iulia Grata Ti Iulii Aug L Mellontis Proc." The slab memorializes Iulia Grata, the wife of Tiberius Iulius Melon, a freedman of the household of Tiberius, who, according to the CIIP editors, was "procurator of the palm groves near Iamnia, formerly the property of Herod's sister Salome, who left it in her will to Livia, Augustus' wife."[80] As procurator of an imperial estate, Iulia's husband would have been responsible for its administration and, likely, the management of its slaves. No term is used to describe the relationship between Iulia and Iulius. The CIIP editors emend the inscription with the word 'uxor' to clarify that she was his wife, this is a strong probability but not certain. Neither is her personal status clear; she is not called 'liberta' of the emperor, her husband or another person.

Khirbet Qumran Ostrakon 1

---

[80] Walter Ameling, Avner Ecker and Robert G. Hoyland, Corpus Inscriptionum Iudaeae/Palaestinae. Volume III, South Coast, 2161-2648 : A Multi-lingual Corpus of the Inscriptions from Alexander to Muhammad (Berlin: de Gruyter, 2014), 166.

Diplomatic Form	See Figure 15.
Transcription	1 בשנת שתים ל בירחו נתן חני ב[ן לאלעזר בן נחמני את הסדי מחול 5 מהיום הזה ל[ע]ול[ם וא[ת] תחומי הבית ו והתאנים הזי[ני]תים וכמלותו ליהד והני 10 לו את חס[די ואת ובית ... ה ל[ ] נן חסדי עבד ח[ני 15 חלון
Translation	1 In year two of [..] Gave Honi son of [..] To Eliezer son of Nahmani Hisday from Holon 5 From today until forever And the boundaries of the house and And the fig trees and the olives And when he fulfills to the community (יהד) And Honi 10 To him Hisday And the And by the hand of (?) Hisday, slave of Honi 15 Holon
Description and Source	Ostrakon among pottery waste at Khirbet Qumran. See

In Book 18 of *Antiquities*, Josephus writes of the Essenes, the sectarian religious community frequently identified with the monastery and scrolls found at Qumran, that they "neither marry wives, nor are desirous to keep servants (δούλων); as thinking the latter tempts men to be unjust, and the former gives the handle to domestic quarrels; but as they live by themselves, they minister one to another."[81] Philo likewise writes of the Essenes, "there is not a single slave among them, but they are all free," δοῦλος τε παρ' αὐτοῖς οὐδέ εἰς ἐστιν, ἀλλ' ἐλεύθεροι πάντες, holding them up as models in his essay *Every Good Man is Free*.[82]

The 1996 discovery at Qumran of a deed of gift involving an enslaved male domestic or agricultural servant, however, has challenged the assumption that the community and its members refrained from the practice of slavery. The Ostrakon, published in 1997 by Frank Moore Cross and Esther Eshel,[83] is a Hebrew inscription comprising 15 lines of fairly legible text, which reads in part: "In year two of [...] in Jericho, Honi son of [...] gave Eliezer son of Nahmani [...] Hisday from Holon," [...]בשנת שתים ל[...] ביריחו נתן חני ב[ן]...לאלעזר בן נחמני[...] את חסדי מחולן[...]; (*bšnt štm l[...] byrḥw ntn ḥny b[n...] l'l'zr bn nḥmny[...] 't ḥsdy mḥwln[...]*) together with a house, fig trees and olive trees, in fulfillment of his "vow to the community," כמלותו ליחד (*kmlwtw lyḥd*). The exact nature of the transaction is further clarified later in the inscription, where Hisday is mentioned as "slave of Honi," עבד ח[ני]. Greg Dounda dissents from this reading, the interpretation of Hisday as a slave, and the reading of 'community' in reference to the Qumran sectarian group, in his lengthy analysis of the fragment.[84] However, while Dounda reads only a hypothetical צ in line 14, I believe that at least the ע and ב of the word 'slave' are clearly readable and consistent with Qumran writing styles.[85]

---

[81] Josephus, *AJ*, 18.21
[82] Francis Henry Colson, tr. *Philo* (Cambridge: Harvard University Press, 1961), 57-8.
[83] Frank Moore Cross and Esther Eshel, "Ostraca from Khirbet Qumran." *Israel Exploration Journal* (1997): 17-28.
[84] Greg Doudna, "Ostraca KhQ1 and KhQ2 from the Cemetery of Qumran: a New Edition," *Journal of Hebrew Scriptures* 5 (2005).
[85] The forms of these glyphs are nearly identical to those of the Isaiah scroll, and could not be mistaken for a צ. See Solomon A. Birnbaum and W. F. Albright, "The Qumrân (Dead Sea) Scrolls and Palaeography," *Bulletin of the American Schools of Oriental Research. Supplementary Studies* 13/14 (1952): 1-52. The chart on page 32 is particularly illustrative.

Figure 15 shows Cross and Eshel's original photo and reconstruction of Khirbet Qumran Ostrakon 1.

Cross and Eshel see Hisday as a personal slave of Honi, a man from Jericho who has made his neophyte profession to the Qumran community, and is deeding his possessions for community use.[86] They suggest that Eliezer ben Nahmani is the "overseer or head of the Congregation," with the legal power to act on behalf of the community and its property.[87] As Cross and Eshel point out, the ostracon is not concrete evidence that the community owned slaves, only that one member formerly did. The fragmentary nature of the end of the document leaves open the possibility that Hisday was freed by the community, or left as a "guardian in charge of the estate" of his former master.[88]

In addition to the biblical texts which recorded earlier Israelite slavery practices, at least one document from the Qumran community anticipates slaveholding. The community whose rule is described in the Damascus Document, found in fragments from Qumran as well in a medieval manuscript tradition including two examples from Cairo, is frequently identified with the Essenes.[89] Verse 11:12 of the document, part of a series of rules concerning the Sabbath, reads in Hebrew: אל ימרא את עבדו ואת אמתו ואת שוכרו בשבת, ('l ymr' 't 'bdw w't 'mtw w't šwkrw bšbt). Ben Zion Wacholder translates the verse as, "One shall not command his man servant, his maidservant or his hireling (to perform tasks) on the Sabbath day."[90] Following this interpretation, the rule can be seen as extending the general

---

[86] Cross and Eshel, 26.
[87] Ibid.
[88] Ibid.
[89] Michael E. Stone, and Frederick Fyvie Bruce. "Damascus, Book of Covenant of," in *Encyclopaedia Judaica*, 2nd ed., eds. Michael Berenbaum and Fred Skolnik, 397-399. (Detroit, MI: Macmillan Reference USA), 2007.
[90] Ben Zion Wacholder, *The New Damascus Document: The Midrash on the Eschatological Torah of the Dead Sea Scrolls : Reconstruction, Translation and Commentary. (Studies on the Texts of the Desert of Judah, v. 56)* (Leiden: Brill, 2007), 91, 332-333.

prohibition on work on the Sabbath to one's servants, a pattern consistent with Exodus 20:10. However David Hamidovič reads ימרא to mean one must not "antagonize, provoke or resist," ones slaves on the Sabbath.[91] The sabbath, according to Hamidovic, necessitates a certain 'gentleness' towards one's slaves, on account of the Hebrews' former enslavement in Egypt.[92] A further verse from the Damascus Document, 12:10 proclaims that a member of the community "shall not sell [to the pagans] his male and female slave who have entered with him into the covenant of Abraham,"[93] ואת עבדו ואת אמתו אל ימכור להם אשר באו עמו בברית אברהם, (w't ʿbdw w't 'mtw 'l mkwr lhm 'šr b'w 'mw bbrt 'brhm).[94] The passage is consistent with the document's overall emphasis on purity, and suggests that, at least for the Qumran community, the distinction between Israelite slaves and foreigners was still operative.[95]

Hisday might have been seen either as an Israelite slave or a Canaanite one. The toponym connected to his name, Holon, corresponds to two known places: the "Holon in the plain of Moab mentioned in Jeremiah 48:21," or alternately, "the priestly city in the hill country of Judea identified by Albright as Khirbet 'Alin."[96] Cross and Eshel prefer the Moabite location, "since it suggests the slave is not a Jew."[97] In fact, both sites are within 20

---

[91] He translates 11:12 as "Que personne ne contrarie son servateur ou sa servante ou bien son salarié le sabbat," with a footnote offering the alternates 'provoque' and 'résiste' for 'contrarie.' See David Hamidovič, L'Écrit De Damas : Le Manifeste Essénien (Collection De La Revue Des études Juives, 51) (Paris: Peters, 2011), 149.
[92] Ibid. "Le sabbat est aussi le jour du souvenir de l'esclavage des Hébreux in Egypte… C'est pourquoi une certaine mansuétude existait ce jour-la pour les serviteurs, les esclaves et les salaries."
[93] Wacholder, 93.
[94] It should be noted that this position extends the biblical provision in Exodus 21, which applies only to males.
[95] Wacholder, 342.
[96] Cross and Eshel, 22.
[97] Ibid.

miles of Qumran,[98] and there is no explicit reason to believe Hisday was not a Jew, apart from the traditional, and incorrect, view that Jews did not hold other Jews as slaves during the Roman period. Either way, the Damascus document shines little light on the final status of Hisday. It contains no rules for the manumission of slaves; neither does it describe communal ownership of them. Neither is it certain that Eliazar ben Nahmani was the leader of the sect. Hezser suggests that he may have been sold, with the money deposited in the "common treasury."[99] I believe it is plausible that he joined the community as an equal. In the absence of evidence, we should trust Josephus and Philo that the Essenes community did not believe in slaveholding, even if they admitted former slaveholders as members. Nonetheless, Khirbet Qumran Ostrakon 1 is important for understanding slavery in early Roman Palestine in several respects. First, it offers concrete material evidence that Jews held enslaved domestic and agricultural servants during the time period. Second, Hisday's inclusion in a deed of gift forecloses the possibility that terms like עבד did not refer to chattel slavery as practiced in the broader empire. Finally, the recency of its discovery suggests that additional realia of slavery may emerge from future archaeological excavations throughout the country.

When taken together, these five inscriptions speak to the social context of slaveholding in first century Palestine. The ossuary of the 'enslaved physician' attests to an owner wealthy enough to keep enslaved persons with a particular, highly specialized skill. The Abu Tor area in which it was found is known for the burials of Jerusalem elite,

---

[98] See Brawer for a description of the proposed locations. Abraham J. Brawer, "Holon," in *Encyclopaedia Judaica*, 497.
[99] Hezser, 292.

including the high priest Caiaphas and his family. Three others, those of the procurator's wife, centurion and imperial freed person, are strongly connected with the Roman civic and military presence in the region. Only the Khirbet Qumran ostracon is indicative of slaveholding by a person of more modest status, and it should be noted that this person likely owned only the single domestic servant described. At least in the first century, the preponderance of epigraphic evidence points to slaveholding primarily by local and Roman political elites.

Chapter 4: Archaeological Evidence

In this chapter I examine two houses of Jerusalem's Jewish Quarter, the 'Burnt House' and 'Mansion House.' Both were destroyed in the First Jewish War; as a consequence they preserve a window into the daily life of Jerusalem's elite ruling class prior to 67 CE. Both sites are preserved today as museums that emphasize their dramatic end, an interpretation that overlooks a long pattern of domestic enslavement supporting a cosmopolitan lifestyle for the city's wealthiest families, from whom the role of High Priest was traditionally selected. Multiple textual traditions maintain that these families were slaveholding; by using this fact as an 'archaeological marker,' we can potentially discover additional details about the extent of slave practices and the way in which they functioned to benefit the region's religious elite.

As Joshel and Petersen point out, slavery is often embedded in the architecture of elite housing in the Roman world. The construction of villas with secure entrances, for example, implicates the presence of doorkeepers, slaves bound to a particular location within the house who often ate and slept there. Elaborate dining spaces and the furniture and tableware that accompany them imply banqueting with carefully choreographed movements orchestrated to re-enforce servility and enhance the master's status in front of guests, frequently fellow slaveholders. Apparatus of containment, including "material remains of chains, shackles, and fetters, as well as literary references to chaining,"[100]

---

[100] Ibid.

remind us of the reality that physical restraint and violence undergird the whole system. A careful examination of these features reveals the ways in which Jerusalem elites lived in an isolated world, with slavery enabling not only their lifestyle but their independent power.

The Kathros House ("Burnt House")

The so-called "Burnt House," which encompassed all of Area B in Nahman Avigad's 1970 excavation of Jerusalem's Jewish Quarter,[101] provides significant insight into enslaved domesticity and activity in pre-revolt Israel. The house almost certainly belonged to the Qatros family, a priestly clan mentioned in the Tosefta (Menahot 13:21) and Babylonian Talmud (Pesahim 57a). Tosefta Minhot 13:21 is a rabbinic "folksong [that] .. relates the corruption of these priests," that twice mentions slaveholding, suggesting that the slaves of these households "beat the people with staves."[102] The Talmud repeats the Tosefta with a minor variation: in the latter, the family is called "Kathros."[103] Among the principal finds at the site was a stone scale weight discovered in Stratum 2 with the inscription "son of Kathros," בר קתרוס, ($br\ qtrws$)."[104] Figure 1 shows the weight as it is displayed at the Burnt House Museum today. Joshua Schwartz lays out the literary and extra-literary evidence for the household's occupants and makes a strong case for connecting it with the one described in the rabbinic sources, despite the considerable passage of time between its occupation and the composition of the Tosefta. He does so partly on the basis of Josephus,

---

[101] Hillel Geva, *Jewish Quarter Ecavations in the Old City of Jerusalem Conducted by Nahman Avigad, 1969-1982. Volume IV: The Burnt House of Area B and Other Studies* (Jerusalem: Israel Exploration Society, 2010).
[102] Nahman Avigad, "How the Wealthy Lived in Herodian Jerusalem," *Biblical Archaeology Review 2: 22* (1976). Online at https://members.bib-arch.org/biblical-archaeology-review/2/4/1. Accessed 4/30/18.
[103] Joshua Schwartz, "Bar Qatros and the Priestly Families of Jerusalem," in Geva, 311.
[104] Ibid., 310.

who writes that, in the time of the high priest Ishmael, "Such was the shamelessness and effrontery which possessed the high priests that they were actually so brazen as to send slaves to the threshing floors to receive the tithes that were due to the priests, with the result that the poorer priests starved to death."[105] If Schwartz is correct, independent literary sources, one contemporary and one from folk tradition, substantiate slaveholding and enslaved activities in support of the priestly functions of the Jerusalem cult in the final years before the destruction of the Temple.

One locus of this activity was almost certainly the "Burnt House" of Area B. This fact allows us to apply a full range of analytical methods to reconstruct domestic slavery in Jerusalem, and the ways in which it might have differed from life in a villa or urban setting in the Western empire. The excavated area of the house is quite modest, consisting, according to Hillel Geva, of "courtyard…, four rooms…, a kitchen…, and a *miqweh*," which may be "part of a larger dwelling that extends to the north and east of the excavated area."[106] The structure was "destroyed by fire during the conquest of Jerusalem in 70 CE,"[107] with substantially all of its contents intact beneath the burn levels and structural collapse. Geva writes that "there are no signs of architectural adornment such as mosaic floors or wall paintings," causing the excavators to believe that "the only rooms of the Burnt House that were exposed were part of the storage and service wing of the house."[108] In other words, the portions of the house preserved for us are the slave quarters.[109]

---

[105] Josephus, *AJ* 20.179-181, quoted in Schwartz, 311.
[106] Geva, 10.
[107] Ibid.
[108] Ibid., 62-3.
[109] A fact which stands in direct contrast with the re-interpretation and presentation of the house by the modern Burnt House Museum, and especially its film dramatization of the destruction. Apart from the Tosefta quotation, the presentation makes no reference whatever to enslaved activity.

Avigad's characterizations of the rooms' utilization is consistent with this conclusion. Since the finds include "an impressive abundance of ... ceramics and stone objects of various shapes and sizes," as well as "many stone weights," one interpretation of the rooms is that they were used in the production of spices or incense for sale to the temple complex.[110] Others, including Schwartz, suggest that the diversity of vessels, including a "volume measurement device,"[111] were used in the collection and distribution of priestly tithes. However, only a moderate number of storage vessels have been found,[112] though 'warehouse' rooms might lay unexcavated in other portions of the site.

More intriguing evidence for industrial activity within the rooms is the discovery of a stone flan mold, used for the production of coin blanks prior to stamping. The mold was discovered in room L.217, a "small rectangular room" which also contained "an installation... of small, kiln-fired bricks," the remains of "many wooden shelves," and a gemstone.[113] Figure 2 shows the flan mold. The location for such a find is so exceptional that Donald Ariel, the project's numismatist, remarked, "one wonders how such an object was ultimately deposited in a domestic context."[114] Numerous coins, also published by Ariel, were found in the room, dominated by those from the Jewish War. However the estimated diameter of the flans is more suggestive of Hasmonean or Herodian coins than those produced by the revolt itself. Still, the mold is potential evidence that the least glamorous stage of coin production, melting and casting of coin blanks, was at one point performed by Qatros household slaves.

---

[110] Geva, 64.
[111] Schwartz, 311.
[112] Fourteen in total, and all in the context of food preparation. See Geva, 134-137.
[113] Geva, 50-51
[114] Donald Ariel, "Coins," in Geva, 245.

Food preparation was also a significant activity in the Burnt House that almost certainly involved enslaved labor. Room L.211 was classified as a kitchen due to the large number of cooking pots and implements found there,[115] but all of the rooms contained two or three stoves. The room also contained a specialized installation including a large stone platter as well as "a pair of basalt grinding stones, ... a stone volume measuring device, ... and a portable stone brazier."[116] The room is only 2.1 m long and 1.5 m wide;[117] as such it is unlikely to have functioned as a household kitchen. Instead, it may have been a space reserved for enslaved persons working in the workshop area to prepare their own meals.

If the rooms now characterized as the "Burnt House" were in fact utilized primarily for enslaved activity, it is important to recognize the role they played in enabling private life and even resistance against enslavement for their occupants, rather than just economic productivity for their masters. Kitchens in general, and certainly slave kitchens, were "out of range of the owner's beckoning," places where, according to Joshel and Petersen, "they could participate in a world largely unknown to the slaveholder."[118] Kitchens and slave workshops could also become hiding places to avoid the physical dangers associated with the lack of control over their own bodies. Slaves might "escape a whipping... avoid work or even... take first step toward flight" through their resort to these "private" slave spaces.[119]

[120]

---

[115] Geva, 33.
[116] Ibid., 60.
[117] Ibid., 66.
[118] Joshel and Petersen, 81.
[119] Ibid., 71.
[120] Joshel and Petersen even suggest that "slaves likely had mental plans of the houses in which they lived, including the places that offered the potential for disappearing from view."

It may be on account of these tactics that tragedy befell one of the final occupants of the "Burnt House." The most sensational find of Avigad's excavation was not the Bar Qatros weight, but the "section of a right upper limb... of a relatively young woman found in the southeastern corner of Kitchen L.211."[121] Baruch Arsenburg assesses her age to be about 25 years and her height to be between 164 and 169 cm. The victim was found "leaning on a stone stair next to the entranceway;"[122] it is unclear whether she was fleeing into or out from the room when she succumbed either to fire or to the building's collapse. It is tempting to characterize the woman as a slave on the basis of the environment in which she was found. While osteology is in some cases helping to connect remains with social status, such a characterization would likely be impossible in this case.

The Mansion House

The structures comprising Area P of Avigad's 1970-1974 excavations, now located beneath the Wohl Museum in the Jewish Quarter, were dubbed "The Mansion House" by him due to their palatial size, comprising over 600 square meters.[123] The central feature of this house is "a magnificent reception hall with white stucco ornamentation arranged in broad panels"[124] and decorated in a purposely archaizing style.[125] The hall, which measures 6.5 meters by 11 meters, is entered from the courtyard on the main level, and is adjoined by three anterooms, all equally decorated. Opposite these rooms, a series of

---

[121] Baruch Arsenburg, "Analysis of the Human Forearm Bones," in Geva, 288-289.
[122] Ibid.
[123] Nahman Avigad, *Discovering Jerusalem* (Nashville, Tenn.: Thomas Nelson, 1980), 95.
[124] Ibid., 99.
[125] Ibid., 102.

windows probably presented visitors to the hall with a view of the Temple Mount and the Mount of Olives beyond.

Avigad draws strong parallels between the wall paintings of the hall and those of the "First Style" and "Second Style" from Pompeii. The opulent decorations of the room are complemented by a wide variety of luxury finds. These include stone tables, such as the ones pictured in Figure 7, as well as an large and ornate mold-blown glass pitcher, bearing the *tabula ansata* of a well-known glass artist from 1st century Sidon, Ennion.[126] The scale of luxury in the home, as well as its prominent position overlooking the temple mount and the large number of ritual baths located within the home led Avigad and his fellow excavator R. Reich to tentatively identify the house with one of the city's high priestly families.[127]

A number of features of the house are suggestive extensive enslaved activity. As described above, the high priestly families were specifically described as slaveholding in the Tosefta and Babylonian Talmud. Unlike the Burnt House, the identity of this particular family is not known, but their home considerably exceeded the size and grandeur of Qathros.' Popular tradition, however, interprets it as the house of the High Priest himself. If this is the case, there is literary evidence to suggest enslaved activity there. Two passages from the passion narrative common to all four gospels, the earliest form of which is roughly contemporary with the structures, describe a "high priest's servant," τὸν δοῦλον τοῦ ἀρχιερέως, (Mark 14:47) and "one of the servants of the high priest," μία τῶν παιδισκῶν

---

[126] Ibid., 107-108, 116-117.
[127] Ibid., 106.

τοῦ ἀρχιερέως (Mark 14:66). The second passage is suggestive that there were several, or many, servants in the household.

Visitors to the mansion house might have encountered slaves everywhere in the space, beginning at the door. Joshel and Petersen identify the role and responsibilities of the doorkeeper in a Roman house, "patrolling access in and out of the house's only entrance," as being well attested in Roman literature, where he is frequently seen as a comic figure drawing parallels with a guard dog at a more modest home.[128] The role of enslaved persons in the security of high priestly households is attested in both the New Testament (John 18:15-18) and Josephus.[129] In the former, servants and temple guards together gather outside the door of the high priest, warming themselves before the fire, while Peter waits with them. This security is, according to Josephus, necessary due to the presence of revolutionary bandits (*sicari*) in the city. These bandits would frequently capture the servants of the high priest, and when taken alive, exchanged in ransom for some of their own prisoners. Thus, slaves of the high priest served at considerable risk to their own personal security despite the privileges their connection to their powerful master would have afforded them. The door itself was likely secured by lock and key; one such was found within the ruins of the house.[130]

Guests entered the banquet room directly from the small courtyard leading from the street, on the house's upper story. Nowhere would the activity of slaves have been more central to the functioning of the Mansion house than in the service and entertainments taking place in the large function hall. The room's overall style and furnishings resembles

---

[128] Joshel and Petersen, 41.
[129] Josephus, *AJ* 20.208.
[130] Avigad, "Jerusalem Revealed," 98.

the dining room of the House of Julius Polybius in Pompeii, which Joshel and Petersen describe extensively in their descriptions of Roman slavery in the context of banquets and dining. The configuration of the house and furnishings of the dining room offer an interesting window into the daily activities of domestic slaves within the architectural landscape. To the diners at the banquet, other slaves would have been both visible and invisible. In such a household, slaves were undoubtedly always "on the move," preparing and serving food, drawing water from the well and cisterns, cleaning up and attending to guests and minor domestic tasks.

Like their Victorian counterparts, domestic servants inhabited the "downstairs" world of the house's lower level, which had no independent access to the street. Though Avigad does not describe a kitchen, it is unlikely that it was found among the frescoed rooms of the upper level. Only small fragments of serving and cooking vessels were found in the rooms of the upper stories. Instead, food was likely prepared in cooking pots downstairs and then plated on tablewares, including those shown in Figure 6, and served to the guests upstairs. The discovery of over 750 cooking pots discarded in a cistern adjacent to the dwelling attests to the volume of food being prepared. In their chapter, "Slavers on the Move in the World of the Banquet," Joshel and Petersen describe the physical efforts and highly-choreographed movements required to carry out table service in an elite Roman context.[131] The strategies in place by slave owners in configuring space for services were often designed to maximize the invisibility and inconsequence of slave activities and reinforce the power structures and give the impression of "food appearing as

---

[131] Joshel and Petersen, 53-59.

if from nowhere."[132] In order to serve guests at the mansion house, slaves would have had to navigate the downstairs rooms and negotiate the staircase leading to the upper story courtyard and the banquet room beyond. Food preparation downstairs was likely both uncomfortable and dangerous due to the smoke produced, the risk of fire, and the added heat in Jerusalem's already hot climate.

Enslaved labor was likely also integral to the ritual purity functions of the household. Food preparation was restricted by the complex dietary rules associated with Jewish observance during an era of increasingly strict adherence. These rules were binding on everyone in the household, even if the enslaved person was not a Judean or otherwise identified with Jewish practices. The presence of stone vessels throughout the Jewish Quarter suggests that the families living there applied halachic rules to the use, cleaning and purification of food implements as well. Avigad suggests this is also the explanation for "35 intact cooking pots... pierced with small holes" and deposited in the courtyard's cistern.[133] The suggestion is that these pots were rendered "unfit for use after they had become ritually unclean."[134]

---

[132] Ibid., 58.
[133] Avigad, 119.
[134] Ibid.

Chapter 5: Literary Evidence

Our principal literary sources for first century Palestine include the various New Testament texts written or set there, the writings of Flavius Josephus, and the community-produced texts from Qumran found among the Dead Sea Scrolls. In addition, the Mishnah and Tosefta, as well as other Early Christian writings, may preserve traditions that go back to the first century. These texts provide a wealth of information about slavery. The New Testament and Mishnah, despite being religious texts, are of particular importance because they represent non-elite voices and, occasionally, voices opposed to the political and social establishment of the first century. An exhaustive examination of the textual tradition is beyond the scope of this project; instead, as described above, I have purposely selected texts that give concrete examples of slavery as it was practiced in the first century in ways that relate to the material record. These texts show, with limited exceptions, the same connection between first century slaveholding and elite social status that is found in the epigraphic record.

Slavery References from Josephus

The collected writings of Flavius Josephus, our primary source for the historical events of early Roman Palestine, contain extensive references to slavery, both in the context of Israel's historical/religious traditions and the contemporary events of his day. Josephus' four main writings, *The Jewish War*, *The Antiquities of the Jews*, his autobiographical *Life* and polemic *Against Apion* together include hundreds of uses of a diverse vocabulary of general and technical terms for enslavement, as Gibbs and Feldman have shown.[135] These uses include frequent reference to Israel's former enslavement in Egypt, frequently as a metaphor for Israel's present subjugation to Rome, or as a counterexample meant to inspire heroic action. Nonetheless, more concrete examples can shed light on the actual historical practice of slavery in the first century.

After rhetorical uses, the most frequent references to slavery in Josephus are the descriptions of enslavements of military captives, usually after the collapse of a rebellion or surrender of a city. Thus when Varus, the governor of Syria, encountered armed resistance from the citizens of Sepporis, he sent his general Caius, who "took the city Sepphoris, and burnt it, and made slaves of its inhabitants," Σέπφωριν πόλιν ἑλὼν αὐτὴν μὲν ἐμπίπρησι, τοὺς δ' ἐνοικοῦντας ἀνδραποδίζεται.[136] The pace of these actions accelerates after the beginning of the revolt in 66 CE. The episode described in *B.J.* 3.10.10[137] is a typical scene. After the surrender of Tarichaea (Magdala) during the Galilean campaign, the citizens are induced to flee to Tiberias, where they are waylaid by Roman soldiers. Vespasian, upon arriving in the city, "stood them all in the stadium," and, having executed the old men and the infirm, "chose six thousand of the strongest, and sent them to Nero, to dig through the Isthmus, and sold the remainder... for slaves," τῶν δὲ νέων ἐπιλέξας τοὺς ἰσχυροτάτους ἑξακισχιλίους ἔπεμψεν εἰς τὸν ἰσθμὸν Νέρωνι, καὶ τὸ λοιπὸν... πιπράσκει. This episode raises interesting implications for the investigation of public forums such as theaters or

---

[135] John G. Gibbs and Louis H. Feldman, "Josephus' Vocabulary for Slavery," *Jewish Quarterly Review* 76, no. 4 (1986): 281-310.
[136] Josephus *BJ* 2.5.1
[137] Josephus *BJ* 3.10.10

stadiums as occasional spaces for enslavement in the Roman period. [138] (Figure 14 shows the theater at Tiberias in 2018.)

In their analyses of the origins of the slave population, both Andreau and Descat and Keith Bradley cite military capture as a principal source of supply for new slaves. In the first century, there was significant demand for new slaves in the Roman empire, and provincial officials acted in response to this economic demand as much as to terrorize their enemies. Bradley attempts to quantify this demand in his essay, "On the Roman Slave Supply and Slavebreeding." He finds that, "for the empire as a whole from 50 B.C. to A.D. 150 in excess of 500,000 new slaves were required each year."[139] Imperial expansion and the suppression of local populations provided a ready supply. Andreau and Descat write, "the laws of war remain constant throughout the periods of Antiquity: the victor has the right to dispose of his prisoners as he wishes, and thus to enslave them."[140] Calling war a "slave hunt," they see significant overlap between military conquest and "banditry, raids and piracy," with the distinction being only the authority of the community carrying out the enslavement.[141] The practice was also entrenched in Roman law and political philosophy, which readily identified servile status with military victimization, where it was seen as a merciful alternative to mass slaughter. Bradley cites as evidence of this "connection between warfare and enslavement" a pair of etymologies found in the *Digest*, "Slaves (*servi*) are so called because commanders generally sell the people they capture and thereby save (*servare*) them instead of killing them. The word for property in slaves (*mancipia*) is

---

[138] The theater at Tiberias has been recently excavated, though the surrounding landscape has not been. It is possible that the remains of the executed prisoners may someday be discovered.
[139] Bradley, "Slave Supply," 43.
[140] Andreau and Descat, 54-55.
[141] Ibid., 56.

derived from the fact that they were captured from the enemy by force of arms (*manu capiantur*)."[142] [143]

Roman law and attitudes toward the legal treatment of slaves is also present in Josephus. In Book 17 of *Antiquities*, Josephus describes the actions taken by Herod in the aftermath of the murder of his brother Pheroras. Poison is suspected, in the form of a drink offered "under pretense indeed as a love-potion... but in reality to kill Pheroras."[144] Herod, enraged, "has some of the enslaved and free women tortured" (δούλας τε ἐβασάνιζε τῶν γυναικῶν καί τινας καὶ ἐλευθέρας), and only after the most extreme methods are applied, obtains confessions of a conspiracy.[145] Peter Hunt, in his chapter on "Sex and Family Life" among enslaved persons, describes one Olympidorus, whose freed *hetaira* "was duped into giving him a 'love potion'... The concoction turned out to be poison... and after his death, she was tortured and executed."[146]

Notwithstanding Herod's reputation for cruelty, there is nothing out-of-the-ordinary in his course of action. That slaves could be, and in some circumstances ought to be, tortured to obtain confessions was a given under Roman law, and one for which there is extensive jurisprudence, which is described by Edward Peters in his book, *Torture*. Peters describes the "absolute right" among owners "to punish and torture their own slaves, when they suspected them of offences against themselves."[147] This right was not infringed upon

---

[142] Digest 1.5.4.2-3. Quoted in Bradley, 44.
[143] The pericope is also fascinating for how it illustrates the way in which mythical etymologies support dominant cultural assumptions. According to Tucker, the primitive meaning of *ser-, to bind, is preserved in the meaning of *servus*, someone in bondage. The later meaning of 'save' is an innovation. See Thomas George Tucker, *A Concise Etymological Dictionary of Latin* (Hildesheim: Verlag Dr. H.A. Gerstenberg, 1973), 221.
[144] Josephus, *AJ* 17.4.1
[145] The story, including the false pretense of a love potion, the conspiracy of free and enslaved women, and their subsequent torture, bears a remarkable similarity to an earlier Athenian account.
[146] Hunt, 104
[147] Edward Peters, *Torture* (New York: Basil Blackwell, 1985), 18.

until at least the third century.[148] The torture of slaves to obtain evidence of a crime was seen as necessary due to their inherent distrustfulness and susceptibility to pressure. Though it was employed as a state practice in serious cases, such as treason against the emperors, Peters shows that "the vast bulk of material in the *Digest* [the compendium of Roman law] in the title 'Concerning Torture' (48.18) refers routinely to the torture of slaves." Keith Bradley believes that torture represented a specific occupational risk for household slaves, who lived in greater proximity to their masters and were "much better situated for picking up incriminating information than non-domestics."[149] This was even more the case in elite households like that of the emperor of Herod's, where slaves might be enticed (or coerced) into participating in the kind of intrigue described above, while being subject to extreme physical consequences.

    The barbarity of routine torture may conceal a more complex relationship between elite persons and slave bodies, especially where deception and intrigue are concerned. In her chapter "Slave Disguise in Ancient Rome," Michele George describes a number of episodes in which elite persons impersonate slaves, or vice versa. These actions could serve to provide security or escape for the master, facilitate sexual license, or even turn a profit. The emperor Nero, George writes, was known to "wander unrecognized through the bars and brothels of Rome with a band of accomplices, thieving from shops."[150] In another instance held up as a more 'noble' example, a slave of the Roman senator Ubinus Panapio "voluntarily put on his master's clothing and ring, lay down in his bed, was mistaken for his

---

[148] Ibid.
[149] Bradley, "Slaves and Masters," 133
[150] Michele George, "Slave Disguise in Ancient Rome." *Slavery & Abolition* 23, no. 2 (2002): 42.

master, and was killed in his place."[151] 'Trading places' represented one strategy that both masters and slaves could employ to their benefit, if they could manage to pull it off. Due to the ethnic diversity of the empire, and to the intermarriage with and outright sexual exploitation of enslaved women by Roman men, it was probably not possible on the basis of general physical appearances to know whether someone was free or slave. It is true that the effects of violent punishment and especially tattooing or branding,[152] may betray slave bodies that have been subject to particularly humiliating abuse. Even this assumption could be exploited, however. Bradley describes an episode in the *Satyricon* in which "the heroes' foreheads were covered with false inscriptions to make authentic their disguise as slaves."[153] George describes the typical slave physiognomy as "ugly and foreign," and suggests that slaves may have suffered "untreated disease or injuries, a lack of proper nutrition," and physical consequences to enforced hard labor.[154]

As another episode from *The Jewish War* shows, Romans believed they could identify these bodily characteristics. In Book 2, Chapter 7, Josephus describes an adopted son of a Roman freedman, a Jew by birth, who bore a resemblance to the late Alexander, one of the sons of Herod put to death by him. This man began impersonating him among the Jewish communities in the Greek world, and raised a considerable fortune by doing so. Caesar himself was able to recognize the fraud for what it was, though, on account of the man's body, the "whole of which was firm and slave-looking," ὅλον σῶμα σκληρότερόν τε

---

[151] Ibid.
[152] Ibid., 47.
[153] Bradley, "Slave and Master," 120.
[154] George, "Disguise," 47.

καὶ δουλοφανὲς.[155] When the deception is revealed, Caesar spares the man, "on account of the vigor of his body," δι' εὐεξίαν σώματος, consigning him instead to row in the galleys.

It is an interesting question whether the specific physical effects of slavery can be identified in extant human remains from the region. To date, no such study has been performed, but promising research from Italy may enable future research in the area. Christian Laes has undertaken an osteology of the 139 new skeletons found at Herculaneum beach in 1982 with the specific objective of identifying the physiological effects of slave labor. He found that at least 32 skeletons, mostly young men but also including women and children, showed syndesmopathies, "serious injuries of the upper muscles," associated with repetitive high intensity activities like tilling soil by hand or rowing.[156] One child of about fourteen, found in care of an infant, showed not only repetitive stress injuries, but significant malnourishment. There is now a significant body of work in support of osteological identification of slavery, including an 1,100 page volume on Pompeii and Herculaneum. Still, Laese is aware of challenges, stating that "it is obviously impossible on the basis of a skeleton to establish whether a person was freeborn or slave, unless one presumes that every slave was marked by hard labor."[157]

Slavery in the New Testament Gospels

Slavery figures prominently in the narrative portions of the New Testament found in the gospels and Acts. A complete analysis of New Testament references to slavery is

---

[155] Josephus, *BJ* 2.7.2.
[156] Christian Laes, "Child Slaves at work in Roman Antiquity." *Ancient Society* 38 (2008): 235.
[157] Laes, 237.

beyond the scope of this project; as the book-length presentations by Albert Harrell[158], Dale Martin[159] and Marion Carson[160] show. Any such treatment will include an extensive analysis of the ways in which slavery functions rhetorically and theologically within these texts as a metaphor to interpret the follower of Jesus as completely devoted to God.[161] It is precisely the prevalence of slavery in Greco-Roman society that makes this rhetoric work: Combes writes, "The metaphor of slavery is a social metaphor... for the most part taken for granted in antiquity. The transference of this relationship to the spiritual plane... is almost as old as the institution of slavery itself."[162]

It is admittedly difficult to bridge the gap from such a purely spiritual metaphor to a form of historical slavery that can be identified through material culture. The metaphor of Christians as "slaves to God" is not the only rhetorical use of slavery in the gospels, however. As Jennifer Glancy outlines in her chapter, "Jesus and Slavery," "the casual frequency of Jesus' reliance on slave imagery is a clue that we should pay careful attention to the slaves and slaveholders who populated Jesus' world."[163] Two recurring tropes within the gospel include the use of slaves as agents or managers, and the rewarding of righteous slaves and corporal punishment of unrighteous ones. In the gospel of Matthew alone,

---

[158] James Albert Harrill, *Slaves in the New Testament : Literary, Social, and Moral Dimensions* (Minneapolis: Fortress Press), 2006.
[159] Dale B. Martin, *Slavery as Salvation: The Metaphor of Slavery in Pauline Christianity* (New Haven, Conn.: Yale University Press), 1990.
[160] Marion L. S. Carson, *Setting the Captives Free: The Bible and Human Trafficking* (Cambridge, UK: Lutterworth Press), 2016.
[161] An in-depth analysis of the way this metaphor functions can be found in the first chapters of I. A. H. Combes *The Metaphor of Slavery in the Writings of Early Christianity*.
[162] Combes, 13.
[163] Glancy, 9.

Glancy identifies six parables that follow this form, in Mt. 13:24-30, 18:23-25, 21:33-41, 22:1-10, 24:45-51 and 25:14-30.[164]

Rhetorical arguments need audiences, and it might be claimed that these slavery metaphors entered the Christian vocabulary as the orbit of early Christianity shifted from Israel to the urban centers of Greece and to Rome itself, and are not reflective of first century Israel. However, slave imagery use emerges from the earliest saying traditions of Jesus and likely from Jesus himself. The parable of the unrighteous tenants, for example, is found not only in the canonical gospels, but in the extra-canonical gospel of Thomas. Glancy writes, "If the figure of the slave were absent from *Thomas*, one might wonder whether the canonical evangelists had written slaves into the parable tradition."[165] [166]

From these gospel parables we can draw several conclusions about slavery in first century Israel that can be instructive in our search for material evidence. First, our confidence that master/slave metaphors and parables go back to Jesus grounds them, as literary sources, in the second temple period. Whatever their connection to the real world, they are not later interpolations and must reflect the understandings of slavery of Jesus' original audience: first century Judeans and Galileans. The basic characterization of slavery in the parables must have matched to some extent with the slaveholding strategies and systems known to his contemporaries. This audience understood, and was comfortable with, encounters with slaves in the context of small agricultural estates, private homes and the marketplace as well as messengers and agents and in the entourage of military and

---

[164] Glancy, 112-113.
[165] Glancy, 106.
[166] Instead, Glancy suggests, the presence of this parable, together with the saying that "no slave can serve two masters," (G. Thom. 65) shows "independent corroboration that Jesus relies on the figure of the slave in his discourse," as do similar parallels found in the first or second-century *Shepherd of Hermas*. See Glancy, 105-6.

priestly officials. Any archaeological context that implicates one of these settings should, I believe, be interpreted in light of the possibility of enslaved activity.

Neither is the New Testament confined to purely rhetorical uses of slavery. In some instances, specific individuals described as masters or slaveholders factor in the narrative as well. While the gospels are not "histories" in any real sense, there has been independent archaeological or extra-biblical literary attestation for a number of New Testament characters, including Herod Antipas[167], Caiaphas[168], Pontius Pilate[169], the apostles Peter[170] and James[171] and the rabbi Gamaliel.[172] The find contexts for the first four of these (the ones with archaeological attestation) correspond closely with the textual accounts. This raises the possibility that, where the New Testament identifies *specific enslaved persons* a particular location, the texts may help contextualize material finds at the site that could assist in the reconstruction of enslaved daily life and activities. Several of these, which I will investigate in more detail, include: the slaves of the centurion at Capernaum in Matthew 8 and Luke 7, and the slaves of Cornelius at Caesarea in Acts 10; Joanna, the wife of Chuza, the ἐπίτροπος "overseer" of Herod in Luke 8:3; Malchus, the high priest's servant in the Garden at Gethsemane (Matt. 26:51; Mark 14:47; Luke 22:51 and John 18:10-11) and

---

[167] In coinage bearing his name minted at his capital of Tiberias. See Jonathan L. Reed, "Herod Antipas in Galilee: The Literary and Archaeological Sources on the Reign of Herod Antipas and Its Socio-Economic Impact on Galilee." *Journal for the Study of Judaism* 38, no. 3 (2007): 203-204.
[168] Through the discovery of his family tomb. See William Horbury, "The 'Caiaphas' Ossuaries and Joseph Caiaphas." *Palestine Exploration Quarterly* 126, no. 1 (1994): 32-48.
[169] By a stone inscription found at the harbor of Caesarea now in the Israel Museum. See Figure 8.
[170] Through graffiti within his purported house at Capernaum. See Robert North, "Discoveries at Capernaum." *Biblica* 58, no. 3 (1977): 424-431. For a more critical interpretation of the epigraphy, that still interprets some epigraphs as 'Peter,' see James F. Strange, "The Capernaum and Herodium Publications, Part 2." (1979): 63-69.
[171] Josephus *AJ* 20.9.1. The so-called James' ossuary is problematic.
[172] Josephus *Life* 38.

tthe maidservant and household servants of the high priest (Matt. 26:69-71; Mark 14:66-69 ; Luke 22:55; John 18:16-26).

The Centurion's Slave

A pair of New Testament pericopes that describe slavery in the context of military officers likely reflects the historical reality of the practice in late second temple Israel. The first of these describes Jesus' healing of the servant of a 'centurion' in Capernaum, one of the principal towns of Galilee, and is found in nearly identical forms in Matthew 8 and Luke 7. The servant (called δοῦλος in Luke but παῖς in Matthew) is described as 'dear' (ἔντιμος) to the centurion. The centurion's entreaty includes a statement about authority in which he claims, καὶ γὰρ ἐγὼ ἄνθρωπός εἰμι ὑπὸ ἐξουσίαν τασσόμενος ἔχων ὑπ' ἐμαυτὸν στρατιώτας καὶ λέγω τούτῳ Πορεύθητι καὶ πορεύεται καὶ ἄλλῳ Ἔρχου καὶ ἔρχεται καὶ τῷ δούλῳ μου Ποίησον τοῦτο καὶ ποιεῖ, "For I am a man under authority, having also soldiers set under my own authority, and I say to this one 'go out' and he goes, and to another 'come' and he comes, and to my slave 'do this' and he does it." (Luke 7:8) This statement confirms, at least as far as the narrative is concerned, that the subject is an enslaved servant, as opposed to a child of the household, and holds a status distinct from the soldiers (στρατιώτας) under his command.

The form of the story itself suggests that it could reflect a historical reality behind the text. Joseph Fitzmyer notes that, "though the episode mentions the cure of a gravely ill servant of a centurion, it is not really a miracle," and that earlier Vincent Taylor sought to classify the episode as merely "a story about Jesus" in which "the interest appears to lie in the incidents themselves."[173] Its inclusion among the Q materials that underlie both Matthew and Mark[174] also suggest a very early date for the episode. Robinson, Hoffmann and Kloppenborg include it in their critical edition as Q 7:1-10, and presume the centurion's speech to be part of the original.[175] In his book *Jesus and the Village Scribes*, William Arnal forcefully argues that the setting of Q accurately reflects the social situation of village life in pre-revolt Galilee.[176] Arnal classifies it as part of Q2, the redactional materials that follow the immediate sayings traditions of Jesus.[177]

The actual office held by the man in question is subject to some debate. Bovon believes that, "since in Jesus' time under Antipas, no Roman troops were normally stationed in Galilee, the *centurio* could only have belonged to the militia of Antipas himself, who also conscripted non-Jewish troops."[178] If this is the case, it may reflect a parallel with the similar story in John 4:46-53, in which a healing is performed for the son of a 'certain royal official' (τις βασιλικὸς). Bovon contrasts his view to that of Marie-Joseph Lagrange, whom he claims, "thinks that a Roman officer could be meant, one who in addition to his regular duties oversees excavations at a mine,"[179] a position I cannot agree with.[180] A local

---

[173] Joseph A. Fitzmyer, *The Gospel According to Luke : Introduction, Translation, and Notes. (Anchor Bible)* (Garden City, N.Y.: Doubleday, 1981), 649.
[174] According to the 'Q' hypothesis, a sayings tradition common to Matthew and Luke preceded both gospels and was independent of Mark. The theory, first advanced by Friedrich Schleiermacher in the 1830s, is widely held by biblical scholars.
[175] Robinson, James McConkey Robinson, Paul Hoffmann and John S. Kloppenborg, *The Critical Edition of Q : Synopsis including the Gospels of Matthew and Luke, Mark and Thomas with English, German, and French Translations of Q and Thomas (Hermeneia: A Critical and Historical Commentary on the Bible)* (Minneapolis: Fortress Press, 2000, 102-117.
[176] William E. Arnal, *Jesus and the Village Scribes : Galilean Conflicts and the Setting of Q* (Minneapolis, MN: Fortress Press, 2001), 202-203.
[177] Ibid., 7.
[178] François Bovon, Helmut Koester and Christine M. Thomas, *Luke 1 : A Commentary on the Gospel of Luke 1:1-9:50. (Hermeneia: A Critical and Historical Commentary on the Bible)* (Minneapolis, MN: Fortress Press, 2002), 260.
[179] Ibid.
[180] On the basis of a complete lack of archaeological evidence for Roman colonial mining activity in the Kinneret region during the late second temple period. This is to be expected, as the region does not possess

connection for the centurion is further supported by verse 5 of Luke's account, in which the Capernaum Jesus followers describe the centurion as 'having built the synagogue for us' (τὴν συναγωγὴν αὐτὸς ᾠκοδόμησεν ἡμῖν).

This local connection offers interesting possibilities for the archaeology of slave life in first century Galilee. A later reconstruction of this synagogue is still standing, and the surrounding houses have been extensively excavated. In the first century CE, situated immediately between the two *insulae sacrae* of the synagogue and St. Peter's house, there stood a block of multi-story dwelling houses that likely served high status individuals of Capernaum. If domestic slavery existed at Capernaum, it almost certainly occurred in the context of these dwellings, including House #1 in Area 2, an unaltered early Roman structure. Figure 9 reproduces Sharon Matilla's plan for the site, together with an inset of its finds; Figure 10 shows my own photograph of what remains of it today. During the early Roman period, the house consisted of a multi-story structure within an enclosed courtyard that also included animal pens, workshops and and a large storage room accessed from the street.[181] The upper story was accessed via an external staircase, still extant. The total area of this house was 317.5 sq. m., and contained as many as 11 rooms.[182]

There are several indications of commercial and domestic activity in House #1 consistent with enslaved labor. Sharon Mattila states that "small-scale commercial

---

any minerals worthy of extraction by pre-modern means. See L. V. Eppelbaum and Y. I. Katz. "Mineral deposits in Israel: A contemporary view." in *Israel: Social, Economic and Political Developments*, Nova Science Publ., NY, USA (2012): 1-41.

[181] Sharon Lea Mattila, "Capernaum, Village of Nahum, from Hellenistic to Byzantine Times." in *Galilee in the Late Second Temple and Mishnaic Periods, Volume 2: The Archaeological Record from Cities, Towns, and Villages*, ed. Joseph Finesy and James F. Strange (Minneapolis: Fortress Press, 2015) 221.

[182] Matilla, 230.

industry.. may also be revealed inside the large House #1 in Area 2, on account of an exceptionally high concentration of ovens found in this house, including two very large ones in one of its southeastern rooms," together with "industrial flour mill of the rotating Pompeian mill ... type"[183] (See Figure 11). For Joshel and Petersen, commercial baking is often accomplished by enslaved persons, due to the intense labor required to produce such a low-cost item.[184] Certainly flour production using the conical Pompeian type was associated with enslaved labor in other parts of the empire. In the days of Plautus, milling was often specifically reserved for convicts and for slaves subject to punishment.[185] In Book 9 of Apuleius' fictional work *The Golden Ass*, the title character Lucius, transformed into a donkey, describes himself as being put to work turning a mill in the company of enslaved laborers, highlighting the extent to which animal labor and slave labor were interchangeable.[186] Apuleius' description corresponds almost exactly with the depiction of flour and bread production on the frieze of the odd and enormous tomb of Marcus Vergiliius Eurysaces, a prominent Pompeii baker and himself a freedman (See Figure 12). Perhaps the owner of House #1 supplemented his income by using the excess labor of his enslaved domestic servants to produce bread and other foodstuffs for commercial sale

---

[183] Mattilla, 234.
[184] Joshel and Petersen, 125-127.
[185] See Ludwig Alfred Moritz, *Grain-mills and Flour in Classical Antiquity* (Oxford: Clarendon Press, 1958), for a list of references to slavery in mills in the works of Plautus. According to Book 3 of Gellius' *Attic Nights*, Plautus himself may have worked in the trade, albeit as an impoverished free man: "Now Varro and several others have recorded that the *Saturio*, the *Addictus*, and a third comedy, the name of which I do not now recall, were written by Plautus in a bakery, when, after losing in trade all the money which he had earned in employments connected with the stage, he had returned penniless to Rome, and to earn a livelihood had hired himself out to a baker, to turn a mill, of the kind which is called a "push-mill."" (Gel. *N. Att.* 3.3.11)
[186] This is a subject that Keith Bradley treats at length in his essay about the *Golden Ass*. See Keith Bradley, "Animalizing the Slave: The Truth of Fiction," *The Journal of Roman Studies* 90 (2000): 110-125.

along the city's adjacent *cardo*. If so, the work would have been particularly arduous in the summer months, when the outdoor heat averaged 36°C (97°F).[187]

While it may be difficult to imagine a hotter or more grueling task for a Galilean slave, at least one less-desirable job did exist within a short distance of House #1. A collection of "scattered pieces of clay hypocaust tiles, both round- and square-shaped, used to raise the floor of the heated room" are evidence of a Roman-style bath house with *caldarium,* existing from the first century and rebuilt in the second or third.[188] It is difficult to imagine these baths being heated and cleaned, or its patrons attended to, except by the use of enslaved labor. In fact, the compilers of the Mishnah, themselves Galileans, assume that the owner of a bathhouse will keep slaves for that purpose. M. Baba Batra 10.6 reports that in the case where two sons inherit a bathhouse, "the rich brother may say to the poor brother, 'buy thee slaves that they may clean out the bath-house.'"[189]

Some of the most remarkable finds in anywhere in Capernaum are the collection of glass tableware identified in House #1, a group that includes matching cruets, bowls and plates from the late first or early second century CE, found lying against a wall at the boundary between Areas 2 and 9[190] (See Figure 9, Inset). While not all fineware is evidence for banqueting supported by enslaved servers, New Testament passages refer to both banqueting and slavery in Capernaum. The house might have supported one or two slaves

---

[187] The macroclimate in the first century was, according to NOAA, comparable to that of the present before the current cycle of global warming that began in the late 1990s. See https://www.ncdc.noaa.gov/global-warming/last-2000-years. The average August temperature for Degania Aleph, the kibbutz on which the Jordan river exits the Sea of Galilee, which was 36°C (97°F) during the years 1961-1990, serves as a good estimate of the region's temperature during the Classical period. See https://www.israelweather.co.il/english/page3.asp?topic_id=82&topic2_id=108&page_id=113.
[188] Mattila, 227.
[189] Herbert Danby, *The Mishnah* (Oxford: Clarendon Press, 1933), 381.
[190] Mattila, 230.

preparing meals, retrieving wine from the storerooms and cleaning dishes at the ground-level well. If dining took place in the upper room (as it is depicted in Mark 14:15 and Acts 1:13), we can imagine slaves ascending and descending the exterior staircase, service materials in hand, with the boundary between upstairs and downstairs serving as a delineator of status.

It is also possible that enslaved labor was associated with the town's most important commercial activity, fishing. Sapir and Ne'eman write that "Galilean fisheries grew in importance especially toward the end of the Second Temple period… when they supported a dense population of over thirty fishing villages… One of the largest in the district was Kfar-Nachum [Capernaum]."[191] These villages were involved in the wholesale capture and processing of freshwater fish for sale further inland. A variety of skilled and semi-skilled laborers would be required for catching, cleaning and salting, as well as maintaining the ships and their equipment. Some of this work was undoubtedly performed by family groups and wage workers, as the account of Mark 1:19-20 suggests. In it, Jesus finds James and John, the sons of Zebedee "mending their nets" in the company of their father and some "hired men," μισθωτοί. However, the Mishnah suggests that, in at least some cases, groups of enslaved persons were attached to particular ships. M. Bava Batra 5.1 states that, "One who sells a ship has sold its mast, sail, anchor, and oars, but he has not sold its [attendant] slaves, nor the packing bags, nor the stores."

The Wife of Herod's ἐπίτροπος

---

[191] Baruch Sapir and Dov Neeman, *Capernaum (Kfar-Nachum): History and Legacy, Art and Architecture*. (Tel Aviv: The Historical Sites Library: The Northern Israel Series, 1967), 7.

Another potentially enslaved person who may reflect historical reality is 'Julia, the wife of Chuza, Herod's steward,' who is briefly mentioned in Luke 8. Bovon writes, "only Luke knows of Joanna, whom he mentions along with Mary Magdalene. The Aramaic name of her husband Chuza is known from Nabataean inscriptions."[192] Bovon states that the term used to describe her husband's position, ἐπίτροπος, means "administrator, governor, overseer," a person who might be "active in the private estates of the princes,"[193] a fact he uses to highlight the privileged status she gave up to follow Jesus. Some parallel uses of ἐπίτροπος from contemporary Roman literature do support that view. For instance, Strabo describes the procurators of Caesar, "men of the equestrian rank, who distribute the pay to the soldiers for their maintenance," ἱππικοὶ ἄνδρες, οἱ διανέμοντες τὰ χρήματα τοῖς στρατιώταις εἰς τὴν διοίκησιν τοῦ βίου, as ἐπίτροποι (Strab. 3.4.20). However, John Goodrich believes that the term, as used here, suggests a Greek translation of the Latin *vilicus*, an enslaved overseer or manager of other slaves.[194] He writes that such administrators were "popularly conceived of as subordinate and servile managers subject to the total (structural and legal) dominance of the master and proprietor.[195] Harold Hoehner identifies specific instances of the term in Judean administration, including "Thaumastus as a manager of Agrippa I's personal estates, and of Syllaeus as manager of the estate of Obadas, king of Arabia,"[196] and quotes Adrian Sherwin-White in saying that the

---

[192] Bovon, 301.
[193] Ibid.
[194] He cites as evidence for this Columella's quote of Cicero's translation of Xenophon's *Oeconomicus* 12.3.4 in his own *De Re Rustica* 11.1.5. See John Goodrich, *Paul as an Administrator of God in 1 Corinthians* (Cambridge: Cambridge University Press, 2012), 72 note 1.
[195] Goodrich, 72.
[196] Harold W. Hoehner, *Herod Antipas* (Cambridge, UK: Cambridge University Press, 1972), 304.

use of the term 'shows the court and establishment of a petty Jewish prince under strong Roman influence."[197]

Conformance to Roman practice would commonly have included the employment of enslaved or formerly enslaved persons in the management of private estates. That is certainly the case with the above-mentioned Thaumastus, since the exact circumstances of his purchase and manumission are recorded by Josephus. In *Antiquities* 18.6.6, Thaumastus is described as originally enslaved to Caius, the grandson of Antonia, when he offers water to the imprisoned Agrippa. In response, Agrippa promises him that, when he himself is freed, he will procure freedom for Thaumastus as well. Keeping his word, he "took particular care of Thaumastus, and got him his liberty from Caius, and made him the steward over his own estate: and when he died he left him to Agrippa his son, and to Bernice his daughter, to minister to them in the same capacity."

Herod Antipas is also known to be a slaveholder from other contemporary accounts. *Antiquities* 19.8.3, records that at the end of Antipas's life, "Herod the king of Chalcis, and Helcias the master of his horse, and the king's friend, sent Aristo, one of the king's most faithful servants (ὑπηρετῶν), and slew Silas, who had been their enemy, as if it had been done by the king's own command." I believe it is extremely likely that Chuza was an enslaved or formerly enslaved household manager for Antipas, and that his Nabatean name may have reflected his origin there or a longer-term connection between his own ancestors, perhaps house-born slaves, and Herod's Idumean forebears. As the wife of an enslaved man or freedman, Joanna almost certainly held the same servile status. Further, there is good reason to believe that both husband and wife are historical. As Hoehner

---

[197] Ibid., 120.

points out, Luke has a special interest in the Herodian family, a fact which "may be due to his acquaintance" with Joanna and with Manaen, another member of the Herodian entourage mentioned in Acts 13.1.[198] [199]

Despite the discovery of an impressive Roman gate, cardo and theater at Tiberias, the remains of Herod's palace there, and the likely workplace of Joanna and Chuza, has not so far been identified. They almost certainly lay somewhere near the base of Mount Bernice within the modern Berko Park, but current excavations there are concerned primarily with Byzantine and Islamic remains.[200] Considerably more remains of Antipas' palace fortress at Machaerus, east of the Dead Sea in modern Jordan and purported site of the execution of John the Baptist. The current excavator, Gyozo Voros, describes it as a "Herodian pleasure palace" which included "a courtyard with royal garden, a Roman-style bath, a triclinium for fancy dining and a formal peristyle courtyard lined with porticoes"[201] (See Figure 13). The sheer size of the structure, which is rivaled only by its sister mountaintop palace at Masada, as well as presence of a triclinium and bath suggest that a considerable staff was necessary for its upkeep. While we cannot be certain that it was made up entirely of enslaved labor, Antipas' use of enslaved servants for higher status functions (described below), probably extended to more mundane roles as well. Undoubtedly, the lost palace at Tiberias would have had comparable levels of enslaved activity. If this is the case, it would situate large scale enslavement directly within the geographic and temporal contexts of the gospel texts.

---

[198] Hoehner, 231.
[199] In fact, Hoehner believes Joanna is the source for the gospel writers' knowledge of the death of John the Baptist. See Hoehner, 120-121.
[200] As was the case when I participated in the 2016 excavations of Tiberias under the direction of Dr. Katia Cytryn-Silverman.
[201] Gyozo Voros, "Machaerus: Where Salome Danced and John the Baptist Was Beheaded." *Biblical Archaeology Review* 38, no. 5 (2012): 37.

The High Priest's Servants

During the arrest of Jesus in the Markan passion narrative (Mk. 14:43-52), an episode repeated in each of the four gospels, a member of Jesus' retinue strike the servant of the high priest (δοῦλον τοῦ ἀρχιερέως), cutting off his ear. The use of the word δοῦλον makes the man's enslaved status unambiguous, and suggests, if historical,[202] that high priestly families of the first century not only held personal slaves, but that they, like those of Herod, were involved in civil matters affecting the temple. According to Jennifer Glancy, the casual way in which the matter is related is suggestive that a first century audience would not find this use of enslaved labor problematic. She writes, "In describing the arresting party, none of the Gospels bothers to mention that slaves are present. Consistent with patterns of narration we find from other sources in the Greco-Roman world, the inclusion of slaves in such cohorts is so ordinary as to escape notice. Had the slave's ear not been severed, no Gospel would note his presence."[203] As invisible as the man might otherwise be, John gives him a name, Μάλχος (John 18:10).

Even less is said of the servants whom Peter encounters in the courtyard of the high priest in Mark 14:53-72. While the other disciples flee, Peter takes up by the fire 'with the underlings,' μετὰ τῶν ὑπηρετῶν (v.54). It is unclear whether these 'underlings' are enslaved, though the Johannine account (18:18) reads δοῦλοι καὶ οἱ ὑπηρέται, 'slaves and underlings.' One of these servants, a young woman, recognizes Peter as part of Jesus'

---

[202] Collins quotes Linnemann in formulating the common view that the episode is taken as historical "biographic apophthegm that Mark uses as a source." (See Adela Yarbro Collins and Harold W. Attridge, *Mark: A Commentary (Hermeneia: A Critical and Historical Commentary on the Bible)* (Minneapolis, MN: Fortress Press, 2007), 685. I take no position on the historicity of the account; I note only that the Markan audience did not see the presence of enslaved persons belonging to the high priest as problematic.
[203] Glancy, 12.

entourage, leading to his famous denial. She is described as "μία τῶν παιδισκῶν," one of the (female) slaves of the household by Mark, suggesting that, in addition to the male servant described above, there are multiple female slaves in the house. The space where they are found, literally, 'below the courtyard,' ἐν τῇ αὐλῇ κάτω,[204] may have been either a permanent place for slaves or a gathering point for them to learn from one another what was going on in the hall. It should be noted that in the case of the 'mansion house' described above, the enslaved spaces are physically located downstairs from the main courtyard.

The Slaves of Acts 10 and 12

Two further episodes from the book of Acts shed light on slaveholding among members the early Christian community itself. The first of these is the account of Cornelius, 'a centurion of the Italian cohort,' ἑκατοντάρχης ἐκ σπείρης τῆς καλουμένης Ἰταλικῆς, described in Acts 10. The historicity of the character is problematic, since, as Pervo points out, "the unit to which he is said to belong was, to the best of available knowledge, not stationed in Judea prior to the First Revolt;"[205] nonetheless he acknowledges the possibility that in the earliest form of the story, the centurion may have been anonymous. Still, Fitzmyer acknowledges that the unit "served in Syria from 69 BC on into the second century AD."[206] This Cornelius sends a delegation to Peter, consisting of 'two slaves and one of his trusted soldiers,' δύο τῶν οἰκετῶν αὐτοῦ καὶ στρατιώτην εὐσεβῆ

---

[204] Various translations render αὐλή as 'courtyard' or 'palace.' The former meaning is more elementary, according to *LSJ*, 276.
[205] Richard I. Pervo and Harold W Attridge, *Acts : A Commentary (Hermeneia: A Critical and Historical Commentary on the Bible)* (Minneapolis: Fortress Press, 2009), 267.
[206] Fitzmyer, 449.

(v.7). The word used, οἰκέτης, can mean any member of the household, but both Fiztmyer[207] and Pervo[208] interpret it as 'household slaves.' As we have seen from the epigraphic evidence cited above, centurions of the first century certainly held household slaves; this episode suggests that they were distinct from enlisted members of the military assigned to serve the centurion. Notwithstanding his slaveholding status, Cornelius is viewed as god-fearing and righteous in the minds of the disciples. Ultimately, 'his whole household,' πᾶς ὁ οἶκός, is converted (11:14) through baptism. Presumably, this household includes the οἰκέται mentioned in v.7. As slaves, the οἰκέται would be expected not only to adopt the religious customs of their masters, but take an active part in the household religion.[209] For this reason, adoption of the family religion could serve the slaveholder's objective "as a tactical approach to integrating the slave and averting flight,"[210] while simultaneously disconnecting them from a religion of birth which might engender collegiality with other slaves and become subversive. Neither was Cornelius expected to free his slaves upon baptism. The Christian community, at least according to Acts, was quite comfortable in his continuing to hold them in bondage rather than threaten the stability of the οἶκός.

The events of the subsequent episode in Acts make this even more clear. Chapter 12 describes Peter's imprisonment by Herod (Agrippa) after the death of James, the brother of John, and his miraculous escape. Verses 11-13 find Peter fleeing to the house of "Mary, the mother of John called Mark." There, he knocks on the door and 'a slave girl named Rhoda

---

[207] Fitzmyer, 451.
[208] Pervo, 258.
[209] Andreau and Descat write, "As for the participation of slaves in household religion... it was customary, but the slave's role was hardly ever described in detail... It is precisely because the slaves' attachment to the family is not is natural as one might think." See Andreau, Jean., Descat, 115.
[210] Ibid.

('rose') comes to answer,' προσῆλθεν παιδίσκη ὑπακοῦσαι ὀνόματι Ῥόδη. Pervo writes, "Mary was evidently a widow of means… since her home was large enough to have an entrance gate and her household included slaves."[211] He further points out that her Greek name stands in contrast to the Jewish names given to mother and son. Unlike Cornelius, Mary and John Mark are core members of the Jesus community who provide refuge and material support within their own home. The presence of an enslaved young woman in Mary's household would suggest that the Christian community saw no conflict between keeping slaves and following the gospel in the immediate aftermath of Jesus' death.

Albert Harrill finds problems with Luke's portrayal of Rhoda. In his essay, "The Dramatic Function of the Running Slave Rhoda: A Piece of Greco-Roman Comedy," Harrill associates the scene with a specific stock figure from Roman comedy: the *servus currens*. He writes, "Far from being a realistic representation that indicates Luke's use of some historical source, Rhoda is a running cliché of Greco-Roman situation comedy. Her function is to intensify the anticipation of the reader, to develop irony … and to provide comic relief at a critical juncture in the narrative when all seems lost."[212] Still, while I admit there are strong literary parallels, I do not discount the possibility that a historical reality underlies the text. Nothing from the epigraphic or literary evidence available suggests that a wealthy Jewish-Christian woman owning an enslaved female domestic servant would be implausible.

---

[211] Pervo, 305.
[212] J. Albert Harrill, "The Dramatic Function of the Running Slave Rhoda (Acts 12.1316): A Piece of Greco-Roman Comedy." *New Testament Studies* 46, no. 1 (2000): 151.

First-Century Slavery in the Rabbinic Tradition

The rabbinic writings codified in the Mishnah represent a third literary tradition distinct from the New Testament and Josephus that can further illustrate the nature of slavery in first century Palestine. While the New Testament is a sectarian religious narrative and Josephus a military history, the Mishnah deals with applications of Jewish law to everyday life, and slavery is a recurring subject. Working with Mishnaic materials is not without challenges, however. Though it makes extensive references to persons and practices of the first century, it is not organized into its final form until approximately 200 CE, and its form makes it difficult to separate out first century materials from later interpolation.

Certainly, the Mishnah includes materials originating in the first century, albeit in redacted form, as well as in continuity between earlier practices and those contemporaneous with its codification: the whole point of the corpus is to preserve oral traditions from earlier rabbis in order to formulate *halakha* in accordance with these previous traditions.[213] Neusner points out, however, that we must rely almost exclusively on the Mishnah itself to tell us about the practices of the first century, a sort of circular reasoning he describes in the introduction to his book, *From Scripture to 70, the Pre-Rabbinic Beginnings of the Halakhah*: "In identifying the starting point in the formulation of any given category-formation with the period before and after 70, I stand on an infirm

---

[213] Benjamin Weiss writes, "The contents of the Mishnah are the product of an ongoing process of elaborating and explaining the foundations, details and significance of the Torah's commandments. This process began long before the redaction of the Mishnah, and continued throughout the Talmudic period." See Benjamin Weiss, "Mishnah." Encyclopedia Judaica, 320

basis. I do not have much evidence outside the documents themselves—the first of them, the Mishnah, reaching closure more than a century after the starting point I allege to locate therein."[214] Still, he believes that "the earliest layers of the laws that ultimately jointed together in the system of the Mishnah rest upon foundations laid forth somewhat before or at the beginning of the Common Era," and that its materials can be identified as originating in one of three periods: pre-70, 70-135 and post 135 CE.[215] The process by which he organizes materials is complex, but he ultimately favors an authentic first century context for materials pertaining to "three points of ordinary life that formed the focus for concrete social differentiation: food, sex and marriage," issues that had the power to define "who was kept within the bounds, and who was systematically maintained at a distance."[216] It is precisely this world of domestic labor and social relations that first century slavery is located; it factors less significantly in the subjects Neusner consigns to later periods, including the Temple and holiness concerns, the observation of festivals, and the institution of Israelite government and politics,[217] though slavery does emerge in matters related to marriage and the marketplace which he locates in the latest (post 135 CE) strand of materials.

Tal Ilan identifies a number of instances where slavery complicates the marital and sexual situation in rabbinic households. M. Abot. 2.7, for instance, quotes the first century rabbi Hillel as saying, "the more maidservants, the more lewdness,"[218] which Ilan interprets

---

[214] Jacob Neusner, *From Scripture to 70 : The Pre-rabbinic Beginnings of the Halakah (South Florida Studies in the History of Judaism No. 192)* (Atlanta, Ga.: Scholars Press, 1998), 20.
[215] Ibid., 21.
[216] Ibid., 232.
[217] Ibid., 232-243.
[218] The same passage which connects 'maidservants,' 'bondwomen' in Danby, with lewdness also connects male slaves, 'bondmen,' with 'thievery.' See Danby, 448.

as acknowledging the reality that "the maidservant, aside from working as a house-servant, is also a sexual object for the males of the house," and that the "sexual exploitation of a defenseless maidservant" was seen as a "lurking danger." [219] The child of such a union would also be enslaved, since betrothal to a maidservant is not valid, a position which was consistent with Roman law.[220] Neither was the exploitation of maidservants confined to free men of the household. M. Tem. 6.2 records the possibility that masters might even induce other slaveholders into compelling their male servants to impregnate a maidservant,[221] presumably with the goal of producing additional enslaved offspring. As Catherine Hezer points out, the Mishnah's goal was not to critique the practice but was "concerned with slave owners' possible involvement in a morally questionable transaction"[222] which might render the fruits of that transaction taboo for use in temple sacrifice.

The presence or absence of slaves in a household could also complicate the prospects of a licit union. Wealthy women were entitled to be free of certain labor if there were maidservants in the household. M. Ket 5.5 records that, a woman who brings into the marriage "one maidservant... need not grind or bake or wash; if two she need not cook or give her child suck; if three, she need not make ready his bed or wool; if four, she may sit [all day] in a chair."[223] The promise of servants later found to be lacking could break an otherwise valid betrothal. M. Qidd. 2.3 stipulates that when a man falsely claims, among other things, "I have a daughter or bondwoman that is a hairdresser,"[224] that the marriage

---

[219] Tal Ilan, *Jewish Women*, 206.
[220] Ibid., 207. Cf. M. Qidd. 3.12 in Danby, 208.
[221] Danby, 561.
[222] Hezser, *Jewish Slavery*, 186
[223] Ibid., 206.
[224] Danby, 323.

contract is invalid. While the legal basis for its inclusion within the Mishnah may have been to illustrate the fact that *any* false claim invalidates a marriage contract, the use of young enslaved women as a hairdressers was likely a common practice. Ilan writes, "presumably those women who could pay to have their hair done could also keep slaves who would do the same thing."[225] Keith Bradley, in his chapter on slave labor in Rome, sees it as a task that could be undertaken by enslaved children after about two months training.[226]

The Mishnah also describes slavery in the context of specific rabbinic households as well as the activities of particular enslaved persons. Catherine Hezser believes that at least some of these traditions go back to a historical reality in the first century. She suggests that, unlike the scholarly groupings of Hillel and Shammai, certain rabbinic 'households' functioned like a Roman *domus*, and that "the priestly houses mentioned in the Mishnah and Tosefta appear in connection with particular Temple-related tasks assigned to them and are likely to have included slaves."[227] She includes among them the "houses of R. Gamliel, R. Shimon b. Gamliel, and R. Chaninah," all of whom are "mentioned in connection with more mundane practices…: the baking of bread, the washing of clothes, the soaking of lentils, and the setting up of candlesticks."[228] In her view, they should not be counted as 'schools' as such, but instead as prominent rabbis possessed of "a slave *familia* which fulfilled certain menial tasks for them."[229]

The house of Gamliel is of particular interest not only because of its connection to the apostle Paul (who was "brought up," ἀνατεθραμμένος, "at the feet of Gamliel," παρὰ

---

[225] Ilan, 188.
[226] Keith Bradley, *Slavery and Society*, 68.
[227] Hezser, *Jewish Slavery in Antiquity*, 126.
[228] Ibid.
[229] Ibid.

τοὺς πόδας Γαμαλιὴλ; Acts 22:3), but because of the Mishnaic references to Gamliel's slave Tabi. Tabi is found in three episodes that show his importance in assisting Gamliel in the observance of Jewish law. In M. Pes. 7.2, he is called upon to "roast the Pesach sacrifice for [Gamliel's household] on a gridiron," an act that would have required specific ritual knowledge as well as culinary skill. During the holiday of Sukkot, Tabi goes missing, only to be found, "sleeping under a bed [in the sukkah]" (M. Suk. 2.1), a ritual practice that is not obligated of slaves. When Tabi finally dies, R. Gamliel receives condolences on his behalf, a practice that is not customary for slaveholders who have lost slaves. (M. Ber. 2.7) Gamliel's students questions him about this, to which he tells them "My servant Tabi is not like all other servants; he is *kasher*," (כָּשֵׁר הָיָה‎, כִּשְׁאָר כָּל הָעֲבָדִים‎ טָבִי עַבְדִּי‎ אֵין‎) a word which means both 'suitable and pleasing' and 'ritually proper.'

The Mishnah passages about Tabi raise fascinating questions about the religious and moral expectations first century Jews had for their slaves. Hezser argues that the stories about Tabi function as exemplars of idealized master-slave relations, a genre that has parallels in contemporary Roman literature. These stories portray a slave "as loyal and obedient to his master, as a model of *fides* and *obsequium*."[230] Keith Bradley believes that there existed a "a repository of such anecdotes about slaves ... generally available to writers,"[231] which found their way into sources as diverse as Valarius Maximus, Seneca and Macrobius.[232] This characterization stands in contrast to the more frequent portrayal of slaves as "dangerous, greedy, dishonest and lazy" found in the works of Roman agricultural

---

[230] Catherine Hezser, "Household Slaves," 395.
[231] Bradley, 33. Cf. Hezser, 395.
[232] Ibid.

writers and the above-mentioned quote from Hillel.[233] In the example of Macrobius, Hezser writes that the slaves of philosophers are "even presented as philosophers themselves."[234] Insofar as rabbinic Judaism represented a "philosophy" in ancient categories, Tabi would be an ideal example of the genre, and one who stands out as distinctive precisely because he defies typical rabbinic expectations that suggested both a general indifference of slaves to *halakha* and an indifference of masters to the plight of their slaves. The very necessity of Gamliel's "explanation" is, for Hezser, evidence that "such behavior was not customary for masters."[235] If this is the case, the picture painted here is somewhat dark: not only do the early rabbinic commentators raise no objections about the ownership of slaves, but are surprised at their dignified treatment.

---

[233] Ibid., 391.
[234] Ibid., 395.
[235] Ibid., 396.

Chapter 6: Conclusions

The evidence of slavery in early Roman Palestine is remarkable in its diversity, however limited it may be in quantity. Enslaved labor was found in elite Jewish households, the courts of local ethnarchs, and among foreign soldiers stationed in the region. Slaves worked on farms, in the banquet halls and ritual baths of priestly families, in public bathhouses and aboard ships, and undoubtedly in a wide variety of other contexts. They served kings, priests and prominent rabbis. They could be physicians, hairdressers, palace guards, estate managers and even body doubles or assassins. At least some married their owners; others were almost certainly buried in their tombs. Given the range of evidence presented, and the strong degree of correspondence with broader first century practice, it may be tempting to view slavery in early Roman Palestine as undifferentiated from slave systems in other parts of the empire. This is not the case.

Almost everywhere where we locate authentic evidence of enslaved labor in first century Palestine, it is connected to the religious, military and political elite. Our epigraphic evidence speaks largely of imperial and foreign military connections, and the places where the literary and material evidence most closely correspond: among the dwellings of the high priestly families, at the various estates and fortresses of the Herodian tetrarchs, and at Capernaum, it is a specific sociopolitical class that exercises slavery. Among all the categories of enslaved activity identified, only domestic service and light commercial activity are found in the broader social context. Table 1, below, summarizes the context and social location for each aspect of first century Palestinian slavery presented:

Table 1: Social Locations of Slavery Practices in First Century Palestine

Slavery Practice	Social Location(s)	Example(s)
Female domestic servants	Priestly households, Herodian households, private households (non-specific)	Mark 14, Acts 12, AJ 17.4, M. Ket 5.5, M. Qid 2.3
Male domestic servants	Priestly households, rabbinic household, unknown	JERU0050, Mark 14, M. Pes. 7.2, Kh. Qum. Ostrakon 1
Banquet service	Priestly households, elite private households	Mansion house, Capernaum House 1
Agricultural overseers	Imperial freedmen, Herodian household, unknown	JERI0007, CIIP III 2268, Luke 8, AJ 18.6, Kh. Qum. Ostrakon 1
Enslaved commercial activity	Priestly household, private households (non-specific); urban communities	Kathros House, Capernaum, M. B. Bat 5, M. B. Bat. 10
Religious observance by slaves	Military household, rabbinic household	Acts 10, M. Pes. 7.2
Violence by or against slaves	Priestly household, Herodian household	Mark 14, AJ 17.4, AJ 19.8

Sexualization of female slaves	Military household, private households (non-specific)	CIIP I.1 734, M. Abot 2.7, M. Tem. 6.2
Slaves as war captives	Military household, Large urban communities	CIIP I.1 734, BJ 2.5.1, BJ 3.10.10
Mass enslavements	Large urban communities	BJ 2.5.1, BJ 3.10.10

The concentration of slavery-related activities in the elite social stratum of first century Palestine should not surprise us. In their chapter on "Slaving as a Historical Process," Del Lago and Katsari emphasize the "creation of anonymous power"[236] as the central innovation of slavery practiced in the context of military conflict and expansion in the ancient world. Such a practice "serv[ed] well the military and priestly elites by building their autonomy on the services of outsiders delivered to them."[237] It is precisely the historical situation of first century Palestine that led local elites and outsiders to depend on slaves for operation and maintenance of the political and religious apparatus. The region was, of course, far from militarily and politically stable. Portions of the region came under direct Roman rule only after the violent collapse of the Herodian dynasty in Judea in 6 CE, and political tensions led to open warfare in the first Jewish War (66-73 CE) and Bar Kokhva Revolt (132-135 CE). During periods of peace, the region was ruled by an uneasy alliance between the high priestly families who held contested religious and moral authority and rulers approved by, or supplied by, Rome. Since slaves were loyal only to

---
[236] Dal Lago and Katsari, 75.
[237] Ibid.

their owners, who had complete legal and physical control over them, they provided an important source of independence and security.

The priestly families controlled the apparatus of the Jerusalem temple, but represented only one faction in the first century Jewish landscape. The Essenes at Qumran denied their legitimacy and emphasized the need for a purification of the temple and land. Samaritans maintained a rival cult at Mt. Gerzim, within the political territory controlled by Jerusalem. Various Galilean groups, including the Jesus movement, also threatened the Jerusalem religious establishment. As a consequence, it makes sense that the high priestly families would rely on enslaved labor to preserve and defend their autonomy against these rival groups. Thus it is no surprise that the strongest witness for the practice of slavery in first century Palestine, attested in archaeological evidence, the New Testament, Josephus and the rabbinic traditions, is found among the elite religious establishment.

Neither is it surprising that local political leaders and the Roman military presence employed slaves. The former were fully integrated into the imperial political establishment; some Herodians even obtained slaves directly from the imperial household, as was the case with Thaumastus.[238] The relationship that these households had with their slaves was one of complex codependency. Antipas counted on slaves like Thaumastus and Chuza to run his household and private estates. But slaves could also complicate dynastic relations and pose a real danger, as the assassinations described in *Antiquities* 17.4 and 19.8 and the impersonation before Caesar in *BJ* 27 attest. Roman military officials, without loyal subjects or allies of their own, undoubtedly relied on personal slaves acquired through warfare for their own comfort and safety.

---

[238] Josephus, *AJ* 18.6.

* * *

It is in this milieu, one that combines limited domestic and agricultural servitude with the broader employment of slavery in support of social elites, that key formative texts and traditions of Christianity and Rabbinic Judaism developed. These texts are engaged in the thought world of slavery in ways that transcend its legal and economic implications. Bernadette Brooten writes in her introduction to *Beyond Slavery: Overcoming Its Religious and Sexual Legacies*, that "slavery had a profound impact on Jewish, Christian and Islamic thinking and laws about bodies, sex and marriage, as well as property and ownership."[239] Without a nuanced understanding of slave systems and practices in early Roman Palestine itself, we risk an incomplete understanding of the broader social, sexual and political context for the West's major religious traditions, even as we attempt to reason from those traditions in search of solutions to modern problems.

In his preface to the volume *Classical Slavery*, a festschrift in honor of classical historian and slavery expert Moses Finley, C. Richard Whittaker wrote that "Finley always felt that ancient history derived its relevance from the possibility of direct confrontation with the modern world, both in its intellectual and political problems."[240] As Peter Hunt points out, interpretations of Roman slavery have left us with an intellectual legacy in the West that remains problematic in a number of ways. The most apparent way in which this occurred was in the arguments made in favor of African-American chattel slavery in the

---

[239] Bernadette J. Brooten and Jacqueline L. Hazelton, *Beyond Slavery: Overcoming Its Religious and Sexual Legacies* (New York: Palgrave Macmillan, 2010), 2.
[240] Whittaker, 3.

19th century. But an Aristotelian logic of "natural slavery" still colors discussions of race and privilege,[241] and Roman law about slavery still impacts modern jurisprudence, especially in civil law jurisdictions.[242] Many current post-colonial issues, especially in Latin America, the Caribbean and sub-Saharan Africa, stem from the harmful attempts to rationalize oppression and cruelty through appeals to the practice of antiquity.

Christians and Jews of the twenty-first century still rely extensively on the ethical and moral norms formulated in first century Palestine in their reasoning about modern questions of justice, freedom and individual autonomy. A recognition of the way in which slavery in that age operated: to preserve and maintain a political, military and religious establishment antithetical to both the Christian and rabbinic traditions, is important when applying reasoning from those traditions to modern questions. But perhaps most importantly, we should continue to examine ancient slavery because it provides us the historical lens to understand how global economic and military practices can engender oppression. As Kevin Bales writes in his book, *Disposable People: New Slavery in the Global Economy*, right now conditions are right for slavery around the world,[243] precisely because of economic globalization and the localized warfare and mass migrations that have accompanied it. It is a situation not entirely dissimilar to the first century. The institution of slavery persists in part because of our ignorance of it: as Bales writes, "everyone knows what slavery is—yet almost no one knows."[244] Expanding our knowledge, not only of the present situation, but the mistakes of the past, is critical to bringing about its end.

---

[241] Hunt, 218
[242] Ibid.
[243] Kevin Bales, *Disposable People: New Slavery in the Global Economy* (Berkeley, Calif.: University of California Press, 2012), 233
[244] Ibid.

www.ingramcontent.com/pod-product-compliance
Lightning Source LLC
LaVergne TN
LVHW020428080526
838202LV00055B/5083